HIDDEN HISTORY
of the
TOE RIVER VALLEY

Michael C. Hardy

THE
History
PRESS

Published by The History Press
Charleston, SC
www.historypress.com

First published 2023

Manufactured in the United States

ISBN 9781467153829

Library of Congress Control Number: 2023937204

CONTENTS

INTRODUCTION

T he history of the more isolated sections of the mountains of North Carolina has not received the attention from historians that it justly deserves," wrote Toe River Valley native Jason Deyton in his master's thesis on the early history of the Toe River Valley. Deyton defended that thesis at the University of North Carolina–Chapel Hill in 1931. Little has changed in the past one hundred years. A second world war has been fought, and mountains once deforested by the swing of the lumberman's axe and the greed of outside interests are now thickly carpeted. Yet the history of the area remains deeply hidden.[1]

Although that history is hidden, it is scattered all around us, just waiting to be discovered. Glimpses can be found alongside the roads we travel and within the communities where we live. Old mica mines that played a crucial role in the victory of the Allies in World War II, convict camps that housed road crews, graves of Revolutionary War veterans and local sites where the Civil War was fought—these hidden glimpses of the past are all around us. While there might not be a sign denoting every site of historic import, history happened right here as well.

The Toe River Valley is composed of Yancey, Mitchell and parts of Avery Counties. We will include all of Avery County in our journey to the region's hidden gems of history. This mountainous area in Western North Carolina has a river system that drains to the west into the Tennessee River and the Gulf of Mexico. The history here is little recorded: a handful of family histories, with more formal studies for places like Mount Mitchell,

Roan Mountain, the Blue Ridge Parkway and Grandfather Mountain. While this project might cover some of the same ground in a few places, it is my hope that there might be a new discovery of something hidden on every page. At the same time, there is so much more work to be done. The Toe River Valley needs dedicated histories of the Civil War and world war years, of mills and schools and of the African American experience from slavery to desegregation.

A handful of people, working at museums or writing where opportunity affords, are this project's foundation stones. It has been an honor since 1995 to be a part of this group, telling the story of the Toe River Valley at sites from the Rush Wray Museum of Yancey County to the Avery County Historical Museum and the Blue Ridge Parkway. I have also been honored to capture fragments of this story through numerous books, like histories of the 58th North Carolina Troops, Avery County, the McElroy House in Burnsville or pictorial histories of Mitchell County, Avery County and Grandfather Mountain. I have also, for over ten years, had a local history column in the *Avery Journal-Times*.

A special thank-you goes out to all of those who showed interest in the project and fielded a seemingly never-ending list of questions: Michael Ledford, Mark Huber, Dan Barron and Jonathan Bennett, along with the staffs at the Rush Wray Museum of Yancey County History, Mitchell County Historical Society and Avery County Historical Museum, as well as Ross Cooper at the W.L. Eury Appalachian Collection at Appalachian State University. A special thanks to my readers, Marsha and David Biddix and Kimberly Wright. And as always, to Elizabeth Baird Hardy, for listening, for tramping the backroads, for reading and for editing. You are the light of my life!

Chapter 1

HIDDEN NAMESAKE

The Legend of Estatoe

There are many different legends regarding Estatoe and the origin of the Toe River's name. This one was taught in Mitchell County schools in 1938:

In the early days before the whites came to these parts, there lived two tribes of hostile Indians. To the east, beyond the Blue Ridge, lived the Catawbas; to the west, among the foot hills of the Unaka Mountains, dwelt the Cherokees. The area that is now known as Mitchell County was rich in Mica, which was used for barter and jewelry. The area was abundant in fishing, and also in hunting. Here the braves met to fight. And sometimes a man and maiden would meet and fall in love. Among the maidens of the Catawba, was the beautiful princess Estatoe, daughter of the Catawba chief. Not unlike the other Catawba women, Estatoe was adept at making jewelry. One day she went out to admire a necklace she had just made in the crystal water of a nearby brook. As she gazed at the stream, she was startled by a sound. She turned to see a young Cherokee warrior. The young brave explained that he had separated from his hunting party and was on his way to meet them. The young Indians found many things to talk about, and their first meeting was a long one. They were both reluctant to return to their tribes and they decided they would meet again. Late in the afternoon would come the distant call of a whippoorwill, and they knew it was time to meet again. Late one evening as Estatoe returned to camp from a meeting with her lover, she paused at the door of her father's lodge. A council was

The North Toe River, about where the Nolichucky River begins, above the Poplar community. *Author's collection.*

in progress and the warriors were giving warning of a hated Cherokee that was lurking near the village. They decided to seek him out and kill him. Estatoe wasted no time in going to warn her lover. Estatoe begged him to escape, but he refused to leave without her. So off they went together. But a sentry followed her, and overheard her plans, and went back to tell the Catawba Chief. The tribe chased them until they were surrounded on a high bluff overlooking the river. Escape was impossible.

The young Cherokee warrior tried to push Estatoe back toward her Kinsmen, but she refused to budge. Placing her hand in his, she stood by his side at the edge of the cliff.

As they stood facing the sunset, they gave a silent prayer to the Great Spirit, then they jumped, hand in hand, from the precipice, far down into the foaming waters. The Catawba chief and his braves approached the spot where the lovers had stood and gazed into the depths below.

He raised his eyes to the heavens, and with arms outstretched, he committed his daughter to the keeping of the Great Spirit. The chief decreed that the river whose waters had enfolded his daughter in death, should be called forever by her name, The Estatoe. The white man later shortened the name to the Toe River, but the spirit of Estatoe lives on in Mitchell County through the telling of this legend.

There are several different variations to this story. In a 1913 version, the relationship between the two young lovers brought war between the factions. Estatoe made a pipe of peace with two stems, and the two chiefs met and smoked until peace was achieved and the sweethearts could marry. Early historian Shepherd Monroe Dugger wrote that the pair were engaged. When her father objected to the union, she drowned herself in the river with her name, "but the whites, being too indolent to hinge their tongues upon the silvery accents, changed the euphonious word to 'Toe.'"[2]

While this romantic story, in all its variations, is lovely, it may not be the "true" origin of the name of the river and its valley. It was not until 1883 that the legend of Estatoe became associated with the Toe River. The story seems to be borrowed from the town of Estatoe in northern Georgia. There was also the Estatoe Path linking the lower Cherokee towns of northwestern South Carolina and northeastern Georgia with the French Broad River. According to an 1845 account, local Native Americans did not even call the Toe River by the name "Toe River," but instead "Calitah," meaning "no value." One historian speculated that Toe either referred to a local family or that the river had several places that had a great tow or undercurrent.[3]

Regardless, the legend of Estatoe, for more than one hundred years, has been adopted by those living in the Toe River Valley, woven into the fabric of local folklore.

Chapter 2

A Little Hidden Geography

Technically, the entire area is known as the North Toe River Valley. Most people leave off "North." The valley is formed by two rivers. The North Toe River has its headwaters in Sugar Gap, between Sugar Mountain and Bald Mountain in Avery County. The river flows southwest through Newland, Minneapolis, Frank, Beech Bottoms, Plumtree, Spear and Ingalls before entering Mitchell County. The South Toe River begins high up in the Black Mountains. The Left Prong of the South Toe River begins between the Bald Knob Ridge and Cherry Log Ridge. The Right Prong of the South Toe River has its headwaters on the Buncombe Horse Range Ridge, not far from Potato Knob. The South Toe River flows through the Carolina Hemlocks Recreation Area, Celo and Newdale. In the Double Island area, the North Toe and the South Toe merge, becoming the North Toe River.

Cane River also has its headwaters in the Black Mountains in Yancey County, flowing through Murchison and Pensacola before emptying into the North Toe River near Huntdale. Above Huntdale, the North Toe River changes names to the Nolichucky River. The Nolichucky runs through the communities of Poplar and Lost Cove, into the Nolichucky Gorge and then crosses into Tennessee. Eventually, the Nolichucky flows into the French Broad and, near Knoxville, joins the Holston River to form the Tennessee River. Some say that the Nolichucky takes its name from an ancient Cherokee village near Jonesborough, Tennessee, and that the word *Na'na-tlu gun'yi* means "Spruce-Tree Place." Others believe that the word means "Rushing Water(s)."[4]

The Toe River Valley can be seen from a popular Blue Ridge Parkway overlook. *Author's collection.*

The Toe River Valley is hemmed in by some amazing peaks. To the south are the Black Mountains. The Blacks form a J-shaped semicircle opening to the northwest and are the tallest mountains east of the Mississippi River. Six of the peaks in the mountain range are over 6,300 feet in elevation. To the north, separating North Carolina from Tennessee from the Nolichucky River to the Watauga River, is the Unaka Range. The Roan Highlands are included in the Unaka Range, and several of the summits rise above 6,000 feet, including Roan High Knob. "Unaka" is derived from a Cherokee word, *une'ga*, meaning "white." Some believe that this refers to the long white blossoms of the America chestnut tree, which once dominated the southern Appalachians; the mountain range turned white when the trees bloomed. South of the Nolichucky River, bordering the North Carolina/ Tennessee line, are the Bald Mountains, named for the many grassy balds. The western side of the Toe River Valley follows a number of points and ridges from the Tennessee state line. Working south, they include Upper Haw Knob, Elk Wallow Knob, Walnut Mountain, Butt Mountain, Sam Doane Mountain, Chestnut Mountain and Cold Knob. The eastern side of the Toe River Valley runs through the middle of Avery County and includes peaks like Sugar Mountain, Loggy Ridge, Spanish Oak Mountain, Little

The Black Mountains were photographed in the 1890s by H.H. Brimley. *State Archives of North Carolina.*

Haw Mountain, Big and Little Elk Mountains, Busk Ridge, Gusher's Knob and Bent Ridge.[5]

On the eastern side of Avery County are three other bodies of water: the Linville River, Elk River and Watauga River. All three have their headwaters on Peak Mountain in Avery County. The Elk River flows west, through Banner Elk and into Carter County, Tennessee, joining with the Watauga River. The Watauga River flows north, into Watauga County. After turning west, it forms the northern boundary between Avery and Watauga Counties before entering Tennessee. The waters from the Elk and Watauga ultimately flow into the Holston River. The Holston River eventually becomes the Tennessee River, joining the Toe/Nolichucky River. Unlike all the others, the Linville River flows southeast. Also bubbling from a spring on Peak Mountain, the Linville crashes over Linville Falls and cuts the Linville Gorge, the "Grand Canyon of North Carolina," on its way to the Atlantic Ocean. After flowing into Lake James, it merges with the Catawba River, then the Wateree River, a tributary of the Santee River. Of course, the dominant feature in the area is the venerable Grandfather Mountain.

Roan Mountain forms part of the Toe River Valley's northern boundary. *Author's collection.*

The Toe River is seen from the Relief community, pre-1968. *Library of Congress.*

Grandfather Mountain is one of the eastern United States' most iconic mountains. *State Archives of North Carolina.*

The Linville River breaks through the Blue Ridge Escarpment at Linville Falls. *Avery County Historical Museum.*

The Watauga, Linville and Elk Rivers all originate from Peak Mountain in Avery County. *Lees-McRae College.*

While not the tallest mountain in the Blue Ridge, its rocky features make it the most distinguishable.

Many of the highest peaks in the area can be visited. Mount Mitchell has been a state park since 1915, the first state park in North Carolina. Roan Mountain State Park is located just across the state line in Tennessee. Much of the North Carolina portion of the mountain is located in the Pisgah National Forest, as is Elk River Falls. Part of Grandfather Mountain is a private attraction, with the Mile High Swinging Bridge, nature area and museum. The backcountry of Grandfather Mountain became a state park in 2009.

There are numerous hiking trails across the Toe River Valley that allow people to explore the geography that tells the ancient history of the area.

Chapter 3

REVOLUTIONARY WAR
AND EARLY SETTLEMENT

M uch of the Toe River Valley was uninhabited at the time of the
American Revolution. The miniature ice age was in full swing, and
living in the beautiful valley was challenging. Samuel Bright was
one of the few settlers who can be documented to the early 1770s. Bright lived
along the North Toe River near the present-day Ingalls community in Avery
County. Travelers heading to the fertile grounds of the Watauga Settlement
could stay with Bright in the "Lower Old Fields of Toe" community until
a large group gathered. They then moved up the old road, called Bright's
Trace or the Yellow Mountain Road, to the confluence of Roaring Creek and
the North Toe River, camping at Upper Old Fields of Toe. From there, the
group moved up Roaring Creek, through Yellow Mountain Gap and back
down into present-day Tennessee. This thoroughfare across the mountains
played a critical role in the American Revolution.

The mountains could provide refuge for those seeking to escape the war.
They could also be dangerous. John Preston Arthur's history of Watauga
County mentions William White witnessing two men "lying out" near
Linville Falls who were killed by Native Americans and their bodies trampled
"beyond site in a mud-hole." Draper wrote in his history of the Battle of
Kings Mountain that Wilkes County's Colonel Benjamin Cleveland sent
"out strong scouting parties to scour the mountain regions, and if possible,
utterly break up the Tory bands still infesting the frontiers." David Hix,
friendly with both dissidents and Tories, had a fort on the Watauga River in
the Valle Crucis section of Watauga County. Benjamin Cleveland attacked

Yellow Mountain Road, or Bright's Trace, was the earliest road carved out of the Toe River Valley. *Avery County Historical Museum.*

the fort, and eventually Hix fled with his family, hiding out for a time near Banner Elk. Another account describes a Patriot scouting group moving through Swannanoa Gap and up the French Broad River before turning east through Ivy Gap and into the Toe River Valley. They continued along the "Caney River," eventually passing back through a gap and dropping into Turkey Cove, McDowell County. According to Annanias Higgins, a member of this group, they "killed and wounded several while they were on this tour" that lasted about four months.[6]

Native Americans used Bright's Trace during the Cherokee War of 1776. British agents encouraged the Cherokees to attack settlements on both sides of the crest of the Blue Ridge. This led to the Siege of Fort Watauga in present-day Carter County, Tennessee, and to raids to the east. Judge A.C. Avery wrote that the "Cherokees came down Roaring Creek to Toe River and crossed…into the North Cove settlement first." In North Cove, or Turkey Cove, the Cherokees raided the farms of the Hunter and McFalls families, scalping both women who lived there but not killing them. Later, Waightstill Avery "passed up Roaring Creek, and hearing the war-whoop behind, spurred his horse and galloped across the head of the creek to the Watauga settlement." Avery afterward ran into a captive woman who had escaped and informed him "that several braves followed him for some distance, and desisted only because they suspected that he was trying to lead them into an ambuscade."[7]

Militia companies from the Watauga Settlements frequently tramped up and down Bright's Trace during the American Revolution. They helped defend Charleston in June 1776 and fought at Fort Anderson and Musgrove's Mill in 1780, at Guilford Court House in 1781 and in Augusta, Georgia. One such action saw hundreds of militia members using Bright's Trace in the fall of 1780. British forces were moving out of South Carolina, hoping to rally Loyalists in North Carolina and defeat the Patriots once and for all. On September 28, the British under Lord Cornwallis entered Charlottetown (Charlotte). Instead of finding a bastion of support, he found a "Hornet's Nest." Protecting Cornwallis's left flank was a force under Patrick Ferguson, chosen to recruit and train Loyalists. Ferguson, who had been skirmishing with small groups of Patriots from various foothill and mountain communities, sent word to the "Over the Mountain Men" that if they did not surrender, he would "march his army over the mountains, hang their leaders, and lay their country waste with fire and sword." Ferguson had already skirmished with Patriot militia as far north as Cane Creek in Burke County.[8]

Ferguson's bold proclamation spurred area Patriot leaders into action. A call went out. Militia men from surrounding counties and from Virginia met at Sycamore Shoals. On September 26, they set out to find Ferguson. The next day, they passed through Yellow Mountain Gap and moved down Bright's Trace, paralleling Roaring Creek, camping for the night in Elk Hollow. They passed Bright's Lower Old Fields of Toe and after "a hard day's march for man and beast…reached Cathey's…plantation…at the mouth of Grassey creek," where they camped for the night. On September 29, the Overmountain Men continued to follow Grassy Creek to its headwaters, where they crossed the Blue Ridge at Gillespie's Gap. Militiamen from the foothill counties of Wilkes and Surry, along with men from South Carolina and Georgia, joined the Overmountain Men at various points. Ferguson's force numbered just over 1,100 men. They took up a defensive position on a small hill just over the South Carolina line, known as Kings Mountain, sending a messenger to Cornwallis for reinforcements.[9]

Patriot forces discovered Ferguson's men at Kings Mountain and attacked on October 7. The ensuing battle was one of the most decisive of

Above: The Old Yellow Mountain Road, used by the Overmountain Men in 1780, was marked by the Avery County Historical Society. *Author's collection.*

Opposite: A monument dedicated on July 4, 1927, to the Overmountain Men was located at Gillespie Gap and has been rebuilt. *State Archives of North Carolina.*

the American Revolution. Loyalist forces were overrun, and Ferguson was killed. The Loyalists lost 290 killed, 163 wounded and 668 captured, with the Patriots losing just 28 killed and 62 wounded. Knowing that Cornwallis was nearby in Charlotte, the Overmountain Men did not linger, retracing their route through the mountains. A portion of the party camped at Davenport Springs on the North Toe River, where Robert Sevier died of his wounds. Sevier, brother to the future first governor of Tennessee, was advised to stay behind and tend to his wound, but fearing capture and imprisonment by the British, he had attempted to make his way back over the mountain. Sevier was buried on October 16 at Bright's Cemetery. While Sevier's is the first recorded White burial in the Toe River Valley, his grave was not marked until 1951.[10]

Thomas Jefferson considered Kings Mountain "the turn of the tide of success." President Herbert Hoover said of the Overmountain Men that a "small band of Patriots turned back a dangerous invasion well designed to separate and dismember the united Colonies. It was a little army and a little battle, but it was of mighty portent. History has done scant justice to its significance, which rightly should place it beside Lexington, Bunker

Hill, Trenton and Yorktown." President Theodore Roosevelt wrote that the victory marked the turning point of the American Revolution. While seldom mentioned, the campaign has an added significance for those living in the Toe River Valley. When those from the Watauga Settlements passed through Yellow Mountain Gap on Bright's Trace, they passed through the highest point connected with the American Revolution. Yellow Mountain Gap is 4,680 feet in elevation. It was in this area that they encountered "snow, shoe-mouth deep" on their way to Kings Mountain.[11]

With the end of the American Revolution came a push to settle the Toe River Valley. According to the terms of the Proclamation Line of 1763, settlement beyond the crest of the Blue Ridge was illegal. This royal prohibition included the Toe River Valley but did not keep settlers in the Watauga Association from leasing land from the Cherokees. It also did not bar some early market hunters, long hunters and settlers, like Samuel Bright, from the area. Following North Carolina's declaration of independence from England in 1776, the land was opened to settlement and land grants, beginning in 1778. Upon taking an Oath of Allegiance to the state, a single man could purchase 640 acres. A married man could purchase 640 acres plus 100 acres each for his wife and each child. Each acre was valued at fifty shillings. The man made a claim on vacant land, and the county courts would issue a warrant; if his claim was not contested within three months, the county surveyor would survey the land and issue a patent. This was sent to the secretary of state, who approved the patent. It took several months, or in most cases at least a year, for patents to be issued. Some of the earliest land grants were issued to John McKnitt Alexander, William Sharpe, Alexander Brevard, Davenport Wiseman, Charles Rease, Samuel Bright, Samuel Harris, Thomas Davenport Jr. and William Tisdall. Waightstill Avery was the largest Toe River Valley landowner in terms of grants, applying for more than 6,500 acres in 1778. Land was also bought from individuals and traded. Some of these men became the first settlers in the Toe River Valley. Others simply engaged in land speculation.[12]

The American Revolution was one of the defining moments in world history. Members of various independent colonies rebelled against British rule, established independent states and, after forming a loose confederation, defeated the most powerful nation in the world. Men who later settled in the Toe River Valley were a part of almost every military action and campaign, from camping at Valley Forge to witnessing the surrender of the British army at Yorktown. Many of them fought at Kings Mountain, the turning point of the American Revolution. The thoughts of these Patriots regarding the debate over the ratification of the federal constitution are unknown. Given their service fighting against government despotism, many were probably leery of giving the government too much power. Hence, the new federal constitution that North Carolina eventually accepted and ratified restricted the role of the federal government in the lives of its citizens.

Chapter 4

Hidden County Formation Histories

I t is not clear exactly when the first Europeans set foot in the Toe River Valley or even who they were. We do know that the Spanish were here in the sixteenth century. In May 1540, famed conquistador Hernando de Soto, with six hundred soldiers, moved from the foothills into the area. One scholar believes that they crossed the North Toe River near the Ingalls community, continuing to follow the river and camping in the Toecane area before moving on into present-day Tennessee. Searching for gold as well as a passage to the West, De Soto found neither. Another Spaniard, Juan Pardo, came at the end of 1566. Pardo and his 125 men established Fort San Juan at Joara, a large Native American village northeast of present-day Morganton in Burke County. From there, they explored for a short amount of time the mountains, once again seeking gold and silver and a way to the mines in Mexico.[13]

Undoubtedly there were hunters in the area prior to settlement. William Linville and his son were killed in 1766 above the waterfall that bears their name. Daniel Boone long-hunted in the area in the 1760s, leaving behind legends of fording the North Toe River at Boonford, as well as camping near Bakersville and on Grandfather Mountain. Samuel Bright, one of the first settlers, applied for and received a land grant for 640 acres on the Toe River in 1778. In addition to his "settlement" of Lower Old Fields of Toe, eight miles north, where Roaring Creek empties into the North Toe River, Bright constructed another "camp" at Upper Old Fields of Toe. Between them ran the already well-worn path only later called Bright's Trace or the

Daniel Boone hunted in the area in the 1760s and 1770s, leaving several local legends. *Library of Congress.*

Old Yellow Mountain Road. A major route for Native Americans moving between the Tennessee Valley and the foothills to the south, it turned north, up Roaring Creek, and crossed the mountain at Yellow Mountain Gap. From there, it was an easy hike into the Watauga Settlement. It was along this same route that James Robertson led a group of sixteen families into the Watauga Valley area in 1771, following the Battle of Alamance. Other settlers came through Gillespie Gap into the Grassy Creek section of present-day Mitchell County, while others followed the "Cane River Indian Trail" into the Yancey County area.[14]

When Bright applied for his land grant, Burke County had just been created. Prior to 1776, the Toe River Valley was loosely part of Rowan County, then the District of Washington in present-day Tennessee. From 1777 until 1792, much of the Toe River Valley remained in Burke County, with Morganton as the county seat. In 1791, Buncombe County was created, and some of the western portions of the valley became a part of that new county. A year later, in 1792, the northern sections of the area were in Wilkes County, and in 1799, that area became a part of Ashe County.

By 1820, there were enough families in the Toe River Valley for residents to begin clamoring for a new county. Travel to either Morganton or Asheville required a ride of several days, and conducting business took considerable time, whether one needed to apply for a license, register new property or serve on a jury. The matter of a new county by the name of Yancey was brought up repeatedly for more than a decade. Representatives from eastern counties did not want new western counties that might vote differently or siphon off money allocated for internal improvements, such as railroads and turnpikes. Repeatedly, the proposed legislation failed. Finally, in 1833, the bill passed the House of Commons by one vote. The new county was named Yancey in honor of Bartlett Yancey, a Caswell County congressman and Speaker of the North Carolina Senate. Casting the tie-breaking vote was Otway Burns, a representative from Onslow County and a War of 1812 privateer. It was rumored that his vote cost him his seat in the next election. In a show of gratitude, the new county seat was named Burnsville in his honor. The land for Burnsville was owned by John "Yellow Jacket" Bailey, and the new courthouse, a log or frame structure, was erected by W.L. Lewis, Daniel Carter, Tilman Blalock, John Edwards and David Baker. The first brick courthouse in Burnsville was not constructed until 1860.[15]

The new Yancey County stretched from the present-day Avery County line all the way to the middle of Madison County. Rumblings for new counties continued. After three years of trying, Watauga County, to the

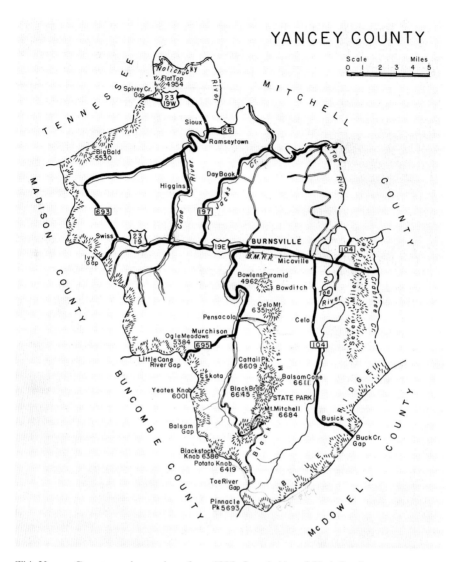

This Yancey County road map dates from 1936. *State Archives of North Carolina.*

north, was created in 1849, encompassing about half of present-day Avery. In 1851, Madison County was formed from parts of Yancey and Buncombe. With the formation of Madison, the Toe River Valley and Yancey County were one and the same. Yet the idea of having a county seat close enough to do business remained a constant idea for residents. It was a long haul from Plumtree or Bakersville to Burnsville. In late 1856, a bill (Number 28) was introduced into the General Assembly titled "A Bill to Lay Off and Establish

Left: Bartlett Yancey served in the U.S. House and as Speaker in the North Carolina Senate, advocating for the formation of a new county. *State Archives of North Carolina.*

Right: A privateer during the War of 1812, Otway Burns served in the General Assembly, voting for a new county. *State Archives of North Carolina.*

a New County by the Name of Avery." The bill was introduced by Yancey County representative Isaac Pearson. Pearson's bill outlined the county that was to be taken from Yancey, Watauga, McDowell and Burke Counties. While the bill gained some favorable votes in the General Assembly, it was eventually defeated.[16]

Burke County representative Tod R. Caldwell introduced a resolution to form a new county by the name of Mitchell in late 1858. It was also "indefinitely postponed" in January 1859. On November 21, 1860, Representative Jacob Bowman introduced yet another bill to establish a new county. The idea that Mitchell County was formed in early 1861 because it was more pro-Union than Yancey County is simply false, a product of stories created, embellished and skewed over time. It took almost five years to create the new Mitchell County, and the concepts for the county were much older.[17]

Mitchell County was named in honor of Dr. Elisha Mitchell, the University of North Carolina professor who was killed measuring the highest peak in the neighboring Black Mountains. For a county seat, the community of Childsville was chosen and renamed Calhoun, probably in honor of South

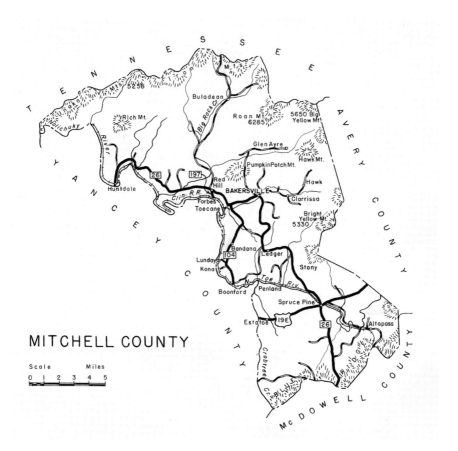

Above: Local communities and geographical features appear in a 1936 Mitchell County road map. *State Archives of North Carolina.*

Opposite: A 1936 Avery County road map shows popular mountains, as well as roads and towns. *State Archives of North Carolina.*

Carolina's John C. Calhoun. A post office had existed in the community since 1850. Childsville/Calhoun, situated where the Avery County Airport/Morrison Field is located today, was not a popular choice. The first meetings of the Mitchell County court were held there in a log building, but by mid-1863, the meetings had shifted to the Bear Creek Church in Ledger.[18]

While there were minor adjustments from time to time, the county lines stayed the same for several decades. In the early 1900s, work began to form a new county out of Mitchell. People living along the North Toe River in the communities of Plumtree, Crossnore and Ingalls were forced to go to Bakersville to attend to legal business. They began to petition their

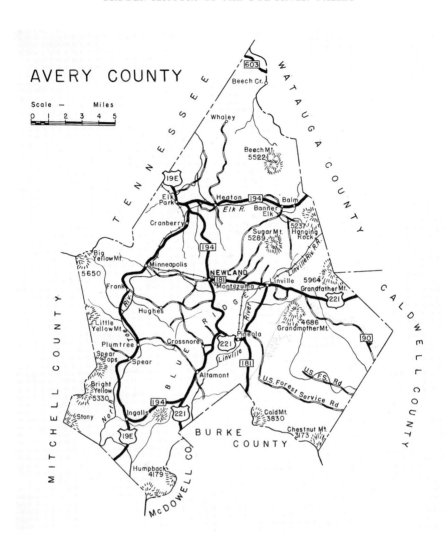

representatives in Raleigh for a new county. In February 1907, J. Clayton Bowman from Mitchell County introduced a resolution into the General Assembly "to establish the county of Park from parts of Watauga and Mitchell counties." The resolution was on behalf of 1,101 local tax-paying citizens. The reasoning was that the area was "enclosed by mountains on the east and west" and plagued by "bad roads from the county-seats of Mitchell and Watauga." At some point, the bill was amended and the name changed to "Hoke County," in honor of former Confederate general Robert F. Hoke. The general was a part owner of the Cranberry Mines. This county formation attempt failed. A proposal for "Appalachian

REV. ELISHA MITCHELL, D.D.

Left: Elisha Mitchell fell to his death in the Black Mountains, attempting to prove that he had measured the highest peak in the eastern United States. *State Archives of North Carolina.*

Right: Will C. Newland served in the General Assembly, was lieutenant governor and ran for the U.S. House. *Avery County Historical Museum.*

County" was introduced in January 1909. This proposal, which took a large portion of land from Burke County, also failed. At the same time, North Carolina senator Robert Doughton introduced a bill to create a new county out of portions of Mitchell and Watauga, named Avery. While there was still much opposition to the creation of a new county in Western North Carolina, the idea, with the help of representatives like Lieutenant Governor William C. Newland, eventually got enough traction to pass in February 1911.[19]

Avery County was named for Waightstill Avery, the first attorney general for the State of North Carolina. He owned immense acreage in the North Toe River Valley area. Newland, the county seat, was named for Lieutenant Governor William C. Newland, who lived in neighboring Caldwell County. Despite several attempts to abolish Avery County through the 1920s and 1930s, Avery County remained, the one hundredth and final county created in North Carolina.

Chapter 5

TREASURES IN THE DIRT

Mining in the Toe River Valley

S pruce Pine: Mineral Kingdom" is how Ashton Chapman described the area in a 1959 article. Chapman was correct. Few areas are as mineral rich as the Toe River Valley. Stories have been passed down for generations of mining by Native Americans and then by the Spanish in the 1500s. Subsequent mining operations obliterated most traces of these early miners. However, mica from Western North Carolina has been discovered in places like Ohio- and Hopewell-era tombs from 100 BC to AD 500. Mica in a museum in Madrid, Spain, is believed to have come from Western North Carolina.[20]

The first post-settlement mining operations occurred at Cranberry. Ruben White, in 1780, discovered a magnetic iron ore seam on Cranberry Creek in present-day Avery County. He filed for a one-hundred-acre grant from the State of North Carolina. This property was acquired by Joshua Perkins, who built a forge in 1820. Perkins applied for a larger, three-thousand-acre land grant, awarded in 1833. He built a dam to supply water for the forge, and his workers hauled the ore in wagons to the site of the dam and furnace. The property passed through various hands. At the time of the Civil War, it was being managed by Jordan C. Hardin, employing several self-proclaimed Unionists who mined iron ore for the Confederacy. After the war, the property transferred to several different groups; it was incorporated in 1873 as the Cranberry Iron and Coal Company, led by General Robert F. Hoke. Part of this company was sold to a Philadelphia group. These interests brought in the East Tennessee and Western North Carolina Railroad and

Cranberry Iron Works smelting furnaces were located by the tracks of the ET&WNC Railroad. *Caldwell Heritage Museum.*

large-scale exploration of the iron ore belt. There were several other iron ore mines in the region, but none as successful as the Cranberry Mine, which closed in 1929—often cited as an example of early southern Appalachia industrialization.[21]

Only after the close of the Civil War did mining endeavors beyond Cranberry gain another foothold. In 1867, Thomas L. Clingman, former U.S. senator and Confederate general, was persuaded to explore mica deposits for New York dealers. Mica is a mineral that crystallizes into very

Laurence Connally, Sink Hole Mile foreman, supervises muck being removed from a shaft. *State Archives of North Carolina.*

thin layers that can be broken apart into thin sheets. Local residents used it for windowpanes in lieu of expensive glass. Clingman reportedly observed this practice when staying at the Silver home near Bakersville. He first mined in Cleveland County and then moved to the Toe River Valley, mining in the Ray Mine in Yancey County and the Sink Hole Mine and Clarissa Mine in Mitchell County. In 1869, John G. Heap and Elisha B. Clapp arrived from Knoxville to mine mica. Their Knoxville Stove Works used the heat-resistant mica for stove windows. Heap and Clapp also worked the Sink Hole and Clarissa Mines, while opening the Deake and Flat Rock Mines. By 1882, at least 400,000 pounds of mica had been mined. Others soon entered the mining field in the Toe River Valley. Thomas Edison, in 1881, developed an electrical motor that used both a mica-laminated armature and a mica-insulated commutator. Mica now had a greater market.[22]

With the arrival of the ET&WNC in 1882 and the Clinchfield Railroad in 1899, mica had an easier route to the nationwide markets. Raymond Jones and Thomas B. Vance erected on Henson's Creek in Avery County the first mica-grinding mill in North Carolina in 1891. Ground mica was used for wallpaper, fireproof roofing and as a lubricant. Jones sold his interest to Vance, who continued the operation with his brother, David T. Vance. Known

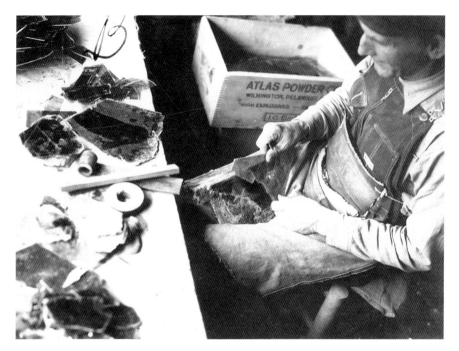

Separating mica into sheets in Spruce Pine was just one of many jobs the industry brought. *State Archives of North Carolina.*

as the "Mica King," David Vance started the Tar Heel Mica Company in 1909. A year earlier, the English Mica Company constructed a grinding plant in Spruce Pine. The mica industry in the Toe River Valley was strong, with numerous mines and companies over the next few decades. However, the Great Depression took a toll, making it cheaper to purchase mica from India. With the eruption of World War II, domestic mica production once again took priority for radios, sparkplugs, transformers and generators. An estimated $150 worth of mica was used in the production of each Allied bomber. The U.S. Geological Survey explored the area in 1940, and a 1942 report claimed that at least 16 million pounds of sheet and punch mica had been shipped out of 131 mines in the Toe River Valley. North Carolina produced three-fourths of all mica used for the war effort. An estimated 2,200 people mined mica, while another 1,500 people were employed "sheeting and trimming" mica. The Meadow Mine in Avery County was reportedly the largest U.S. mica mine. Another prominent mica mine was the Isom Mine on Celo Mountain in Yancey County, first opened in 1874 by the Silver brothers and known as the Cattail Mine. With the mine entrance at five thousand feet, it is the highest mine in the eastern United States.[23]

A load of feldspar is removed from a Mitchell County mine in 1939. *State Archives of North Carolina.*

Mica mining declined after World War II, but in the 1950s, there was once again increased demand as the United States became involved in the Korean War. A grading facility was built in Spruce Pine under the auspices of the General Services Administration. The plan was to purchase twenty-five thousand tons of mica within three years. However, the program was still running through 1956. A 1967 map, prepared by the Department of the Interior, marked 707 mica mines in the Toe River Valley, plus an equal number of unnamed prospects.[24]

Kaolin is a soft white clay used in the manufacture of china and porcelain. The arrival of the Clinchfield Railroad provided a way to transport kaolin to market. The Edgar brothers of New Jersey opened a mine in Penland, while the Sparks Plant opened in Minpro, both in 1908. The C.J. Harris plant in Ingalls opened in 1937. Howard Marmon was co-owner of this company when the name was the Kaolin Corporation. The company was sold numerous times, including to the Unimin Corporation, which is now owned by SCR-Sibelco of Belgium. Kaolin is no longer mined in the Toe River Valley.[25]

Feldspar was first used as a cleaning agent, but over time, additional uses were found, largely in the glass-making industry. The North State Feldspar Corporation and the Feldspar Milling Company both had plants in Micaville beginning about 1911. There were eventually numerous mines: Mitchell County's Chestnut Flat, Flat Rock, Deer Park No. 1 and Sugar Tree Cove Mines; Avery's Water Hole Mine; and Yancey's Gouge Rock Mine. Half of the feldspar being produced in 1929 in the United States was coming from the Toe River Valley. Feldspar was used in Bon Ami Cleaning Powder and was mined at the Bon Ami Mine, known locally as the McKinney Mine, near Little Switzerland. Many mines also produced quartz (silicon), used in electrical devices that include semiconductors, and the Spruce Pine pegmatites are considered the purest quartz in the world.[26]

Numerous other rocks and minerals have been mined in the Toe River Valley over the past two hundred years. There are gold mines on Grandfather Mountain, and Thomas L. Clingman mined silver in northern Avery County. The Estatoe community has the Crabtree Emerald Mine, possibly mined by Tiffany and Company of New York at the end of nineteenth century. One 6.5-pound emerald from this mine was purchased by the Smithsonian in 2016. There were several uranium prospects in the area, but the quantities of this element are small. Graphite, used as a lubricant, as well as in batteries and in pencils, was mined in the Busick community of Yancey County. Mining employed many local people and was important to the local economy for generations.[27]

Chapter 6

MOUNT MITCHELL

History Hidden in the Clouds

Rising 6,684 feet above sea level, the Black Mountains can be seen from downtown Burnsville, Grandfather Mountain and the Roan Mountain range. They dominate the surrounding countryside for miles in every direction. For centuries, the Black Mountains served as a boundary between the tribes of the Cherokees to the west and Catawbas to the east. Both tribes probably hunted throughout the range. Some believe that the Cherokees referred to the Black Mountains as *Gv-na-ge-i*. Spanish explorers Hernando de Soto and Juan Pardo passed by the Black Mountains in search of gold or a shorter route to the silver mines in Mexico. English explorers arrived a century later, men like James Needham and Gabriel Arthur from Virginia, attempting to establish trade with the Cherokees. Once the Toe River Valley was officially open to settlement, scientists like Frenchman André Michaux and Scotsman John Fraser made their way to the Black Mountain range.[28]

While the high reaches of the Black Mountains held little attraction for settlers, they drew scientists in droves. Probably the most famous was Dr. Elisha Mitchell. Reared in New England and a Yale graduate, Mitchell became professor of mathematics and natural philosophy at the University of North Carolina in 1818. Several years later, he inherited the Geological and Mineralogical Survey, authorized by the North Carolina General Assembly. From Grandfather Mountain, which he scaled in mid-July 1828, Mitchell could see Yellow Mountain, Roan Mountain and, to the west, the Black Mountains. "It was a question with us whether the Black or Roan

Mountains were not higher than the Grandfather," Mitchell jotted in his diary, adding that he suspected the "Black and Roan to be higher peaks."[29]

For decades, many believed that New Hampshire's Mount Washington (6,288 feet) was the highest peak in the eastern United States. Some started to question that assumption, and in 1835, Mitchell set out to measure Grandfather, Roan and the Blacks. Using a barometer, Mitchell measured Grandfather and Roan. The Black Mountains remained a challenge due to the numerous peaks. He measured Celo Knob, then Yeates Knob (now Big Butt) and another unnamed peak, surveyed in the clouds. Mitchell returned in 1838 and 1844 to take additional measurements.[30]

Thomas L. Clingman, U.S. senator and Confederate general, mined and promoted the Toe River Valley. *Library of Congress.*

Controversy soon swirled around who had measured the true highest peak. Thomas L. Clingman—a former student of Mitchell's, amateur geologist and U.S. congressman—with numerous business ties to the Toe River Valley, was certain that Mitchell had measured the wrong spot. Clingman visited the Blacks in 1855, believing that he had ascended and measured the correct peak. Correspondence was exchanged between the pair, with Clingman believing that Mitchell's 1844 visit did not lead the professor to the highest peak. Mitchell was quite certain he had measured the highest peak during his 1835 visit. The debate turned public when Mitchell turned to an anti-Clingman newspaper in Asheville with a series of letters and pamphlets. Clingman responded in turn in a rival newspaper. Mitchell returned to the Black Mountains in 1857 to reevaluate his earlier explorations and measurements. On June 27, 1857, he set out to interview William Wilson, one of his 1835 guides, and to possibly preach in the Cane River settlements. The professor never made it. When he had not arrived by the following Wednesday, search parties set out from the Swannanoa Valley and from the Cane River settlements. Mitchell's body was finally discovered by Big Tom Wilson on July 7, 1857, in the pool of a forty-foot waterfall.[31]

It was eventually determined that Professor Mitchell had truly measured the highest peak in the Black Mountain range. In 1858, the high peak, Black Dome, was renamed Mitchell's High Peak and then later Mount Mitchell, in

Mitchell Falls is featured in a circa 1857 lithograph published by Oscar M. Lewis. *Wilson Library, University of North Carolina–Chapel Hill.*

his honor. The creek and waterfall where he fell to his death are also named for him, as are Mitchell Ridge and Mitchell County. The Yancey County group that found the professor's body carried it to the top of the mountain, intending to bury him there. The Buncombe County group disagreed. Mitchell was buried first in Asheville, but a year later he was reinterred on the peak that bears his name, on a piece of property donated by Jesse Stepp. Professor Mitchell still rests on the top of Mount Mitchell.[32]

The debate between Mitchell and Clingman is just one part of the history of Mount Mitchell and the Black Mountains. At fifteen miles in length and shaped like a fishhook, the Black Mountain range includes six of the ten tallest peaks in the eastern United States and boasts several impressive records: the lowest temperature ever in North Carolina, -34 Fahrenheit, recorded on January 21, 1985; the largest snowfall ever recorded in North Carolina in a twenty-four-hour period with thirty-six inches on March 13, 1993; and wind speeds as high as 178 miles per hour.

Tourism was in full swing by the 1850s. The Mountain House was constructed in 1851 on a trail from the town of Black Mountain to the various peaks. Other cabins and campsites were spread across the ridges and slopes, including at Stepp's Gap. In 1873, the National Weather Service constructed a weather station on Mount Mitchell, but it was destroyed by fire. Thomas L. Clingman spearheaded the interest in local mica mining along the Black Mountain range in the late 1860s, attracting others, like Garrett Ray. With businessmen finding uses for mica, this led to other mines, such as the McKinney Mine, Sawnee Hill Mine, Whitson Mine and Bill Autrey Mine, often named after the men who owned the property or operated the mine.[33]

While selective logging had taken place from time to time, the boom of the early 1900s brought large-scale deforesting to the Black Mountains. In 1912, nine thousand acres in Buncombe County were sold to a logging firm. Work was soon underway on a railroad to access the large stands of Black Mountain range timber. By 1914, the railroad reached within a half mile of the summit of Mount Mitchell. Trees were loaded onto logging cars and moved down the mountain to a mill in Black Mountain. There were more than a dozen logging camps around Mount Mitchell. Most disappeared after the timber was cut.[34]

On the Toe River Valley side of the mountain, three lumber companies sprang up. The Philadelphia-based Carolina Spruce Company was situated in Pensacola and timbered a 5,200-acre tract. Also from Pennsylvania was the Brown Brothers Lumber Company, which logged the 13,000-acre

The Old Mount Mitchell Trail, circa 1920, was photographed by William A. Barnhill. *Library of Congress.*

Left: Governor Locke Craig grew up exploring the Black Mountains and pushed to see a park established. *State Archives of North Carolina*.

Below: Elisha Mitchell was originally buried in Asheville and then re-interred atop Mount Mitchell one year later. *Author's collection*.

tract known as the Murchison Boundary. Its headquarters was the Eskota community. The Chicago-based Mount Mitchell Company had a nine-mile section of land along the upper reaches of the South Toe River. All three companies laid their own rail lines to their stands of timber, while utilizing the Black Mountain Railroad to export milled timber to Kona, connecting to the Clinchfield Railroad and outside markets. Between 1880 and 1924, an estimated 90 percent of the forests across the South were lost to timber companies. The boom years came during World War I. Timber from the Mount Mitchell area was used to build airplanes. After the Great War ended, the logging industry slowly decreased.[35]

As widespread logging was deforesting the Black Mountains, the Weeks Act, passed in 1911, authorized the establishment of national forests in the eastern United States. The bill allowed the federal government to purchase "forested, cut-over, or denuded lands within the watersheds of navigable streams deemed necessary for regulation." In 1913, the U.S. Forest Service purchased property in the area that became some of the foundational properties of the Pisgah National Forest.[36]

Governor Locke Craig, elected in 1912 as the fifty-third governor of North Carolina, said in an address at Black Mountain, "When I look upon that mountain and see the havoc wrought by the woodsman's axe, I feel like a citizen of Rome who gazed upon his city burning and in ruins. I cannot but regret that it is not as it was." Under Locke's administration, the State of North Carolina purchased property on March 3, 1915, passing a bill establishing Mount Mitchell as North Carolina's first state park. The state purchased 525 acres along the ridgeline, from Big Tom to Stepp's Gap. Half of the property had already been logged. In 1918, the state purchased an additional 700 acres of deforested property. By 2023, Mount Mitchell State Park encompassed 4,789 acres. In honor of Governor Craig's advocacy, the second-highest point in the Black Mountain chain was renamed Mount Craig in 1947.[37]

Chapter 7

EDUCATIONAL TREASURES

Lost Schools of the Toe River Valley

O ver the past two centuries, numerous schools have appeared and vanished in the Toe River Valley. North Carolina enacted the first statewide common school law in 1839, combining local and state funds for public school support. A statewide tax was instituted in 1869, providing for a four-month school term. Governor Charles B. Aycock led the charge to remake the state's school system, and between 1900 and 1910, more than three thousand new schools were built in North Carolina. Other modifications came, lengthening the school year, adding grades, requiring standards for teacher qualifications and specifying which subjects were taught. Starting in the 1920s and 1930s, the national educational scene began to change. There were calls for a common, national school system. The local community schools, dominated by families and the church, gave way to centralized schools. While the local schools and educators had sometimes been ill-equipped, families were often directly involved. When the state-mandated schools were found lacking, some sought alternate educational opportunities by creating additional educational institutions. The long-gone Toe River schools described here are vital pieces of the past.

BURNSVILLE HIGH SCHOOL/YANCEY COLLEGE, YANCEY COUNTY

Citizens of Burnsville founded, under the auspices of the Methodist Church, the Burnsville High School/Burnsville Academy in 1851. Milton P. Penland was chairman or president, and S.D. Adams was the first headmaster. The coeducational school had a five-month term. John W. McElroy offered boarding to female students; male students could board in town. By April 1853, the school was being advertised across the state in various newspapers, having the "most modern and approved Text Books," a planetarium, a tellurium and chemistry lab equipment. No photograph of the school exists, although an 1853 advertisement stated that male and female recitation were held in separate buildings. Adams had been replaced by Reverend Thadeus P. Thomas by 1854, and an advertisement appeared in Raleigh stating that the upper grade levels were now Yancey College, with dormitories being erected. What became of Yancey College is unknown, and it appears that the buildings were burned in the last few months of the Civil War. Perhaps Burnsville Academy was a separate school that grew from the postwar ashes of the Burnsville High School. In 1886, J.J. Britt was listed as principal of the Burnsville Academy.[38]

THE WING ACADEMY AND GOOD-WILL LIBRARY, MITCHELL COUNTY

Like many people, Charles H. Wing chose to retire to the Toe River Valley. Born in 1836 in Boston, Massachusetts, Wing was a Harvard graduate who taught chemistry at Cornell University and the Massachusetts Institute of Technology. Wing moved in 1885 to the Ledger community of Mitchell

Professor Charles Wing, who founded a Mitchell County library, is buried under a pyramid at Bear Creek Church. *Author's collection.*

The Good-Will Free Library was located in the Wing Community, Mitchell County. *State Archives of North Carolina.*

County, constructing a school and furnishing supplies, teachers and a free education including the basics, as well as classes such as carpentry and sewing. That first year, there were 250 applicants. Wing also founded the first free public library in North Carolina, the Good-Will Free Library with twelve thousand volumes, most of them discarded from a Boston library, sent by northern friends. Wing built a two-story structure housing the library and, on the second floor, a meeting room for "civic and social gatherings." He also constructed a cottage nearby for the librarian. Wing went a step further, establishing small traveling libraries. Each box contained seventy-five books transported via wagon. Wing passed away in Massachusetts in 1915 and is buried at the Bear Creek Baptist Church Cemetery in Ledger. The library was donated to the Mitchell County Board of Education, which placed the books in various school libraries.[39]

BOWMAN ACADEMY/MITCHELL COLLEGIATE INSTITUTE, MITCHELL COUNTY

Several members of the nineteenth-century Bowman family were educators. James C. Bowman founded the Bowman Academy in Bakersville in 1890.

The Bowman Academy/Mitchell Collegiate Institute was founded by James C. Bowman and sold to the Baptists and then to the county. *Robert Morgan.*

Bowman ran the subscription school for a number of years, but by 1897, he had decided to sell the facility. One Asheville newspaper reported that in 1899, the Baptists in Mitchell County were trying to raise the necessary funds. One month later, they had a contract and were planning to open the new term on September 1. The school was renamed the Mitchell Collegiate Institute and, in 1917, had 117 students, with both girls' and boys' dormitories for boarding students. The Mitchell Collegiate Institute was sold to the Mitchell County Board of Education in 1923, which renamed the facility Bakersville High School. Later, it was renamed after J.C. Bowman. An elementary school building was added in 1926, and in 1936, the high school building was replaced. This building mysteriously caught fire in 1940 and was replaced by a stone structure in 1942. In 2023, Bowman Middle School occupied the ground.[40]

AARON SEMINARY, AVERY COUNTY

The Eastern Continental Divide runs from Calloway Peak on Grandfather Mountain southwest, through Avery County. Streams to the west, including the Toe River Valley, drain into the Gulf of Mexico. To the east, streams flow into the Atlantic Ocean. Aaron Seminary sat almost astride the Eastern Continental Divide in the Montezuma community. Like many of the other higher-level schools in the Toe River Valley in the late nineteenth and early twentieth centuries, Aaron Seminary was founded and funded by a church, the Methodist Episcopal Church. The nonsectarian, coeducational school opened in the fall of 1891 in a building accommodating two hundred students, two literary societies, a music department and business courses. Aaron Seminary's brush with fame came in 1903. In Boone, Edward F. Lovill was recruited by brothers Blanford and Dauphin Dougherty to help petition the General Assembly regarding a northwestern North Carolina state-supported institution to train teachers. Lovill had already pushed through such a bill in 1883 while serving in the General Assembly. The first school in Boone was short-lived,

Montezuma's Aaron Seminary was the only place, besides Boone, receiving votes to become a teachers' school in the early 1900s. *Aaron Seminary Annual, 1900–1901.*

moving to Sparta in 1887. One of the provisions of the new bill was a meeting to be held to determine a location. At the meeting in Blowing Rock were representatives from Ashe, Wilkes, Caldwell, Watauga, Mitchell and Yancey Counties. Everyone agreed on the location in Boone except the representatives from Mitchell County, who cast votes for the Aaron Seminary in Montezuma. Boone, the location of the Watauga Academy, won. The school eventually became Appalachian State University. Aaron Seminary continued for a few years, but the annual report for 1915 noted that the "old Aaron Seminary building has been taken down."[41]

Yancey Collegiate Institute, Yancey County

In September 1899, delegates of the Yancey Baptist Association, meeting at Crabtree Baptist Church, decried the "poor condition, inadequate equipments [sic] and short term of our public schools." They pledged to do something about the situation. By the next annual meeting, the association had announced that it had raised about half of the funds to build a coeducational Baptist high school in Burnsville. Work was nearly completed by the next year, and the school was scheduled to open on September 9, 1901. In 1903, the school applied for a charter from the state. Dormitories were constructed, along with an administration building that was replaced after a fire in 1918. The school advertised classes in science, music and home economics, an athletic field and a library with 1,400 volumes. The school was located on Parnell Hill, overlooking the town of Burnsville, and had an enrollment of three hundred students. When the state began offering high school, enrollment decreased, and in 1925, the property was sold to the county for use as a public high school. Two of the original buildings survive: the Brown Dormitory for Boys (1914) and the second Administrative Building (1919). The county then added several buildings over the next decades, including a gym that became the Parkway Playhouse. In 2003, the Yancey Collegiate Institute Historic District was added to the National Register of Historic Places.[42]

Stanley McCormick Institute, Yancey County

In 1898, the Home Mission Board of the Northern Presbyterian Church established the Stanley McCormick School in Burnsville, named in

Stanley McCormick Institute was operated by the Northern Presbyterian Church in Burnsville from 1898 to 1926. *University of North Carolina–Chapel Hill, Wilson Library Special Collections.*

honor of the son of benefactor Nettie McCormick of Chicago, widow of inventor Cyrus McCormick and generous education supporter. The coeducational school had a library and infirmary and offered courses in science, mathematics, agriculture, wood and iron working, shorthand, bookkeeping, music, religion and history. Extensive buildings were constructed for classes and dorms in Burnsville. The school was considered "A Practical Life School" and originally included all grades, but the elementary grades were later removed to focus on more "mature" students. In 1926, the McCormick family turned over the funding of the school to the Presbyterian Church, but the church was unable to keep the school open. One newspaper considered the failure of the school a "calamity." There was an attempt for a few years to keep the school open, and in 1927 the organization received a new charter as Carolina New College. In the summer of 1929, the college was rented by the communist Southern Summer School for Women Workers in Industry, which trained about forty "rank and file" women millworkers for six weeks in economics, labor history and public speaking. Several of the women were involved in a strike in Marion in October in which six male strikers were killed by local law enforcement. It is not clear who fired first. The November trial of the strikers was moved to Burnsville. Four strikers were tried for rioting, found guilty and sentenced to work on the public roads. The officers involved were also tried but found not guilty. Carolina New College struggled on for a few years, closing in 1931. Several of the buildings survive today.[43]

LEES-MCRAE BOYS SCHOOL/PLUMTREE SCHOOL FOR BOYS, AVERY COUNTY

Sent by the Presbyterian Church in the summer of 1895 to the Banner Elk community to plant a church, Reverend Edgar Tufts found a bustling community with a hotel, post office, two general stores, a Methodist church and a school. He returned the following year, and the new church was dedicated in August. In 1897, Tufts married and returned to the community, where he began pastoring local Presbyterian churches and inviting young people from the community to read classical and popular literature. Before long, they had put together a small library that became the nucleus of a school, and the upstairs room was converted into a classroom. Soon, students started coming from the surrounding areas, boarding in town. Tufts gained permission from the Concord Presbytery to establish a formal school. In 1900, the Elizabeth MacRae Institute (as it

The Lees-McRae Boys School/Plumtree School for Boys was the counterpart to the Banner Elk girl's school. *Author's collection.*

was spelled at the time) opened. With new buildings and benefactors, the school grew, and with growth came a name change. The school became Lees-McRae Institute in 1903. Lees-McRae Institute was a school for girls. A school for boys was opened in Plumtree as early as 1903 by Reverend J.H. Hall. In 1907, Hall reported that he was educating 150 young men. The early school was called the Lees-McRae Institute for Boys. Students were instructed for the ministry, but over time, the school also became a military school. The name was changed to the Plumtree School for Boys in 1922, operating under its own board of trustees. The school was plagued by fires. One in 1908 destroyed the main dormitory, and the boys lived in tents until another building was completed. In January 1927, the main dormitory again caught fire. A spark from the furnace caught the shingle roof ablaze, and 60 students lost everything. Later that year, the Holston Presbytery decided that instead of rebuilding the boys' school, the male students would be moved to Lees-McRae Institute. In 1930, the school became known as Lees-McRae College. Only one of the buildings of the Plumtree School for Boys survives.[44]

Higgins Neighborhood Center, Yancey County

The John and Mary R. Markle School of Industrial Art was not a typical school. Instead of teaching the three Rs, the school taught needlework, weaving, basketry and woodworking. The industrial school was held in the Higgins Neighborhood Center in the Higgins community. Pennsylvania native Martha E. Robison, the impetus behind the facility, arrived in January 1922, a missionary for the Board of National Missions, Presbyterian Church (North), with a goal of completing a community center and home for a resident missionary. A scheduled three-month job became a lifetime appointment. Robison oversaw the building of the Sunshine Cottage (which later burned and was replaced by a stone structure), a new Presbyterian church and Kirksedge cottage. There was also a craft store where local students could sell their handiwork. Robison served as executive secretary of the organization for seventeen years. A medical clinic was established in the facility. In 1950, the facility was purchased by the Seventh-day Adventists, who continued the clinic. It was the only such structure for miles around. The Higgins Clinic remained open through the 1950s.[45]

Neighborhood Center
Higgins, N. C. Federal Route 19 W

Higgins Neighborhood Center in Yancey County taught woodworking, basketry and needlework and later was a medical clinic. *University of North Carolina–Chapel Hill, Wilson Library Special Collections.*

Chapter 8

THE CONFESSION OF FRANKIE SILVER

There are a few stories that ripple across the fabric of North Carolina history. Sir Walter Raleigh and the lost Roanoke Colony, the adventures of Blackbeard the pirate, Orville and Wilbur Wright's first flight at Kitty Hawk and the Greensboro sit-ins are just a few narratives that capture people's attention. Another piece of North Carolina's past, often crossing the boundary from history into folklore, is the poignant tale of Frankie and Charlie Silver, a young couple who lived near the North Toe River in the present-day Kona community in the early 1830s.

The grim story of the short lives of Charlie and Frankie (Frances Stewart) Silver is well known. Books (both fiction and nonfiction), stage plays and even musical compositions have been written about the tragic events. Yet Frankie supposedly left a seldom-referenced confession of the events that transpired in December 1831. This confession was printed in the *Southern Citizen* in February 1837, almost four years after her death. Is the confession truly hers? Some disagree that these are her actual words. The piece is well written and not expressed in the vocabulary of a teenage girl from an isolated mountain community, a girl set to be executed for the murder of her husband. While someone else undoubtedly set pen to paper, there are some compelling descriptions of the area found within the confession.

In the purported confession, Frankie tells us that she married Charlie in October 1828. They had only been married three months when they began to quarrel. Instead of working around their homestead, Charlie took his gun and dogs and went hunting. A relative had confided in Frankie

The Kona Methodist Church, closed circa 1940, stood across from the church cemetery where Charlie Silver was buried. *Michell County Historical Society.*

that Charlie was "sporting and hunting," living off a relative that was "a cripple." When confronted, Charlie, holding a rope, responded, "Damn you if you take his part instead of mine. I will put you to an end." Later that week, when on their way to visit a neighbor, Charlie ordered Frankie to return to their home, stating that if she did not, "he would sacrifice me in the road." Charlie then pushed her down and ran off. Frankie confronted him the next day, saying that she "had left her father and had taken him for my friend." Charlie told her that "he was not my friend, neither did he intend to be, but wished I would go back to my father or friends and remain." Charlie then left, swearing that "he would not return until I left." Frankie did leave, going to Charlie's uncle's house. Charlie returned that evening, and they made "peace."

These events all occurred while they were living in Buncombe County. The couple moved "over on the Toe River" shortly thereafter, near the present-day community of Kona, and "lived friendly two or three months." Charlie came home one evening stating that he had been persuaded to leave her. He then "commenced whipping the teeth of the card that I had in my lap. I then told him he acted as if he had not good wit." "[D]amn you," he replied, "I thought I could make you mad after a while. After which very rough and ill language passed from each to each one…he pushed me out of the door, struck me one or two blows and drew off of me one side of my frock." Frankie ran off to Charlie's father's house. Returning that evening, she found his gun and clothes gone. "I then began to cry, and he heard me and come up to the house and told me, damn you, I had no intention to leave you; but I done it to try your pluck, to see if you loved me, and by that have found out that you do." For a time, the couple "lived in peace, but finally we began to dispute, and several little disputes took place, and at different times." They argued over clabber set on the dinner table, an argument that turned abusive when he struck her and threw her out of the house. They again patched things up, but soon thereafter they fell out again. This time, Charlie took a knife to bed, "with the intention to kill me," Frankie confessed. She waited until he was asleep before removing the knife from under the pillow.

Several weeks later, Charlie just up and left without giving reason, staying away for three weeks. She moved out of their cabin. When Charlie returned, he asked her to move back in, and she agreed. Their daughter, Nancy Silver, was born shortly thereafter. Things really did not improve. "Various times we differed and as often did he threaten me with death," she asserted. "Very many times has his treatment towards me been reprehensible & insufferable." On one occasion, as they returned from a church service, "he was mad & threatened me with death, he took down his gun and snapped it at me twice without being replied to in any way." On another occasion, Frankie asked him to build a fire and he refused. She told him he was lazy, and then Charlie "struck me one blow that fractured my rib." There were several other events of abuse outlined in her confession.

One evening in December 1831, they had a row over flax, who was responsible for building the fire and sweeping the woodchips out of the cabin. Charlie punched Frankie and then grabbed an axe nearby, "swearing at the same time that one or the other must *die* before day." Charlie then laid down the axe, picked up his gun and commenced loading it, saying, "Damn you, I will shoot you." While he was getting a bullet out of his shot pouch, Frankie discovered that his attention was "off of me, and I immediately pitched at the axe, got hold of it, and struck him one blow with the pole of the axe, and he fell, and as he struck the floor I struck him one more blow.…I then threw down the axe, and for a few moments was insensible to every thing." Charlie died about an hour later. "I thought if I could only call back the lick I would give ten thousand worlds," Frankie admitted. Not knowing what to do, Frankie confessed, "*I just rolled him into the fire*, whole as he was,

Charlie Silver's body parts were found at different times, hence the three graves and gravestones at the Kona Baptist Church. *Author's collection.*

without touching him with any edge tool and did not cut him up." She threw in several "bushels of big hickory chips…he burnt the whole night," while Frankie "washed all the blood off the floor" and then her clothes. Frankie then went to Charlie's father's home and then to Buncombe County.[46]

After several days, people began to look for Charlie Silver. Fragments of bone and blood under the floor of the cabin were eventually discovered. Frankie Silver was arrested for his murder. The trial began in Morganton in March 1832. She was convicted of the crime, and after an unsuccessful escape, on July 12, 1833, she was hanged in front of thousands of witnesses. With the summer heat, her family was unable to carry her remains back up the mountain, and she was buried at the Giles-Devault Farm Burial Ground outside Burke County. Parts of Charlie's body were found at different times and were buried beside each other. Hence Charlie Silver has three graves at the Kona Baptist Church Cemetery, Mitchell County. Many people feel that Frankie was the victim of not only an abusive husband but also poor legal advice. Burgess S. Gaither, then clerk of court, believed that had she admitted to killing him and pleaded self-defense, she probably would have been found not guilty.[47]

In 1886, "Frances Silvers' Confession" began to make the rounds in local newspapers. It was reportedly a ballad that Silver wrote right before she was executed. Henry Spainhour, who was working in Lenoir at the time of the trial and execution, disputed the idea that Frankie had penned the lines. Instead, an acquaintance of his, Thomas W. Scott, had written the confession, modeling it on another ballad known as "Beachman's Address." The latter ballad told of a murder and execution in Frankfort, Kentucky. "Frances Silver's Confession," better known today as "The Ballad of Frankie Silver," was almost certainly not written by Frankie Silver as she awaited execution in a jail in Morganton. Definitively proving that the 1837 "confession" is a forgery is a harder task. It was published just four years after her death. The greater question yet to be solved is how the editor of the *Southern Citizen* acquired details regarding the case.[48]

Chapter 9

CIVIL WAR HISTORY IN THE TOE RIVER VALLEY

Undoubtedly, the 1860s are some of the most misunderstood years in the history of the Toe River Valley. It is often said and repeated that Mitchell County was formed because it was pro-Union, that Mitchell County had the area's largest group of Union soldiers and that Montraville Ray, who led the Burnsville Raid, was a Unionist. Not one of those statements is true. A campaign for the formation of Mitchell County began at least six years prior to 1861. As a gauge of Unionism in the Valley, Yancey County sent more men to the Federal army than Mitchell County did. Montraville Ray was just a part of a group that seldom gets mentioned, a third group wanting nothing to do with either side during the prolonged war. The history of the Civil War in the Toe River Valley is a complex and hidden piece of local history.

SECESSION AND EARLY ENLISTMENT

Wars are always started by politicians and newspapers. While the Toe River Valley had no local newspapers at the time, citizens could learn from more regional newspapers of the growing hostility in the mid-nineteenth century. America was a deeply divided country. The Whig Party believed in a strong federal government, with higher tariffs to support transportation infrastructure, economic development and businesses. In the 1850s, the Whig Party collapsed. Some former Whigs joined with radical abolitionists to create the Republican Party. The Republican Party in 1860 was

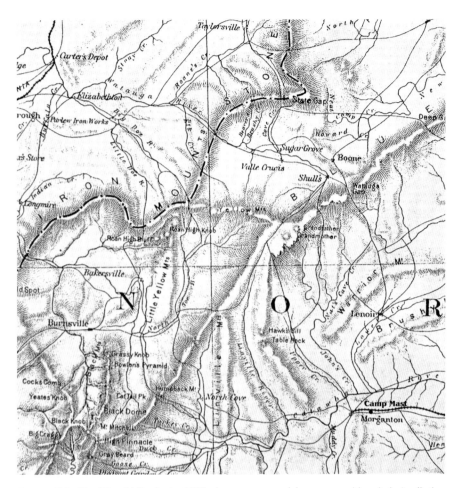

A map of the Toe River Valley in the 1860s shows many surviving communities. *Author's collection.*

a regional party with little support in the South. In opposition was the national Democratic Party. Known as the party of the "common man," the Democratic Party supported individual rights and state sovereignty and was opposed to government-controlled banks and high tariffs. If a power was not proscribed by the federal constitution to be considered on the federal level, then the power was left to the states. The Toe River Valley had typically voted a strong Democratic ticket during many of the mid-nineteenth-century elections.[49]

The men elected to represent the Toe River Valley in the General Assembly in Raleigh were strong states' rights advocates. Governor John W. Ellis told the state in his annual address in 1860 that "the Republic has at last fallen upon those evils against which the Father of the Country so solemnly warned us in his parting advice." A national election had just been held. Local Toe River men had voted overwhelmingly for Democratic vice president John C. Breckinridge for president. With a fractured Democratic Party, the winner of the national election was Republican Abraham Lincoln, who did not garner enough supporters to even earn a slot on the statewide ballot. Many states in the Deep South began to call for conventions to consider secession from the Union. The idea of secession was nothing new. States in New England had clamored for disunion since 1794. Marcus Erwin, who represented much of the Toe River Valley in the state senate, was seen wearing the "blue cockade of secessionist" when he arrived in Raleigh in November 1860. Not long after the General Assembly met, Erwin submitted a bill calling for a convention of the people of North Carolina to consider what direction the state needed to take regarding the election of the Republicans. W.W. Avery, whose family owned large tracts of land along the North Toe River, also submitted a similar bill. Back in the Toe River Valley, Congressman Zebulon Baird Vance was hanged in effigy during court week in Burnsville in January 1861. Vance was a conditional Unionist, believing that North Carolina needed to support the Union until the Republicans actually did something unconstitutional.[50]

On January 29, 1861, a bill was passed to call a convention to consider the question of secession and to elect delegates. Both Erwin and Jacob Bowman, in the North Carolina House, voted in favor. Between the call for a convention and the actual vote, the General Assembly passed the bill establishing Mitchell County. It had taken six years to establish the new county. Even with its creation—with its own magistrates, justices of the peace, sheriff and court officers—the county would continue to vote with Yancey County until after 1865. When the votes were tallied after the February 28 call to consider a convention, the two counties had just barely voted against calling the convention: 556 for and 598 against. Statewide, the margin was just as close: 46,672 for and 47,269 against. While the Toe River Valley voted against the call for a convention, the region did elect Milton P. Penland, a "pronounced secessionist after the election of Lincoln," to represent them should the convention have taken place. He beat local Unionist J.W. Garland.[51]

Lincoln's inaugural address in April 1861 did nothing to alleviate the situation. One historian argued that it actually made "secessionists of many conditional Unionists." North Carolinians, including those in the Toe River

Valley, began to mobilize for war. Lincoln then contradicted his word, sending troops to Fort Sumter in Charleston. On May 13, just over one hundred men from the Burnsville, Ledger and Day Book areas gathered in Burnsville, enlisting in the Black Mountains Boys, electing James S. McElroy captain. This group of men became Company C, 16th North Carolina State Troops. That same day, local men gathered to vote again on the idea of calling a convention. The vote passed, so Penland headed to Raleigh, where, on May 20, he voted to repeal the ordinance of 1789, which had ratified the Constitution of the United States, dissolving the union between North Carolina and United States. The delegates in Raleigh then ratified the Constitution of the Confederate States of America. A little more than a week later, Isaac Avery was in the Toe

North Toe River property owner W.W. Avery represented part of the area in the statehouse and Confederate Senate. *North Carolina Museum of History.*

River Valley recruiting. Like his brother W.W. Avery, Isaac owned property in the area. Many of Avery's men came from the North Toe River Area, becoming Company E, 6th North Carolina State Troops. Both the 6th and 16th Regiments were sent to Virginia.[52]

Other men continued pouring out of various communities to enlist in the Confederate army. Company B, 29th North Carolina Troops, under the command of Captain William Creasman, was composed of men from Burnsville, Paint Gap and Egypt. Captain John C. Blalock commanded Company I, 29th North Carolina Troops, with men from the environs of Bakersville, Spruce Pine and Fork Mountain. The men in Company G, 29th North Carolina Troops, came from Ramseytown, Day Book and Egypt areas and elected Melchizedek Chandler captain. Bacchus S. Proffitt was elected captain of Company K, 29th North Carolina Troops, with men primarily from Burnsville, Bald Creek and Egypt. At the end of 1861, yet another company was raised. John B. Palmer was appointed commander of the Mitchell Rangers, created in response to the bridge-burning episode in east Tennessee, and his men came from the North Toe River area around Linville Falls, Childsville, Pyatt, Crossnore and Grassy Creek. By the end of 1861, almost eight hundred Toe River Valley men had voluntarily enlisted in the Confederate army.[53]

CONSCRIPTION

Most men volunteered to serve one year. As that year ended, the Confederate Congress passed a Conscription Act, requiring men between the ages of eighteen and thirty-five to remain or join the army. The Conscription Act was passed on April 16, 1862. Men were given a five-month grace period to enlist in a chosen company before being forced into the army and assigned where needed. Several new Toe River Valley companies were organized in the interim. Jacob Bowman organized a company of men from the Fork Mountain, Red Hill and Bakersville areas. William Proffitt organized another company of Day Book and Burnsville men. Mexican-American War veteran John C. Keener began raising yet another company, partially from the Bakersville and Fork Mountain areas, although many of the men came from Caldwell County. John W. Peak's company was composed of soldiers from Day Book, Egypt and Burnsville. Samuel M. Silver raised the final Confederate infantry company from the valley. His men largely transferred from Keener's company. Samuel English raised a cavalry company from the Childsville and Yellow Mountain areas. The infantry companies became the nucleus of the 58th North Carolina Troops, with Palmer promoted to colonel. English's cavalry company became a part of the 5th Battalion North Carolina Cavalry. Both organizations left the Toe River Valley, fighting in Tennessee and Georgia.[54]

A small handful of local men crossed through the mountains into Kentucky to join the Federal army. This was a long, perilous journey. In August 1862, several young men gathered at the home of George Dugger in the Banner Elk community. Those men included John Lineback; brothers Columbus, Oliver and Newton Banner; and their cousins Samuel and William Banner, Henry Tatum Banner and Joel Eggers. Eggers, William Banner and John Lineback joined the 4th Tennessee Infantry (U.S.), while Oliver, Newton, Henry T. and Columbus Banner enlisted in the 4th Tennessee Cavalry (U.S.).[55]

John B. Palmer moved to the area in 1858 and commanded the 58th North Carolina Troops and the Department of Western North Carolina. *North Carolina Museum of History.*

The war began seeping into the Toe River Valley communities. The justices meeting in court in Burnsville at the end of the year complained that so many men had enlisted in the Confederate army that it was now dangerous to call additional men out for regular service. Several times the local militia had been mustered and sent to neighboring Madison County to deal with thieves and bushwhackers. In another instance, Palmer was attempting to buy cattle for his troops along the Linville River when he was accosted by Jeremiah Oaks, who attempted to shoot Palmer. When Oaks's pistol misfired, Palmer took out his pistol and killed Oaks. The following year was little better, with more trouble in the Shelton Laurel community of Madison County and countless problems with deserters from both armies and dissidents roaming the mountains and hollers. These desperados had attacked the home of Melchizedek Chandler, threatening his wife with hanging. At least three men were killed in a skirmish at Henry Roland's house on Jack's Creek in July 1863, and a raid took place at the Avery home in Plumtree in October.[56]

HOME GUARD

Into this fray entered the Home Guard. With most of the militia gone, serving in the Confederate army, there was a dearth of law and order. Governor Zebulon B. Vance had attempted to use what remained of the militia to enforce Confederate conscription law, but the North Carolina Supreme Court ruled against him. Instead, Vance and the General Assembly created the Home Guard in July 1863. Local militia colonel John W. McElroy was tapped to command all the Home Guard battalions in the western part of the state. The militia and the Home Guard were two different organizations. At times, McElroy's headquarters was located in Burnsville and at other times in Madison County. Yancey County was designated as the 72nd Battalion North Carolina Home Guard, with Samuel D. Byrd promoted to lieutenant colonel and placed in charge. Mitchell County apparently never completed a Home Guard company or battalion organization. A few from the greater Banner Elk area served in the 11th Battalion North Carolina Home Guard. Anyone exempt from the Conscription Act was liable for service in the Home Guard. Unfortunately, most of the Home Guard records for the Toe River Valley evidently did not survive the war. The Home Guard was assigned to seek out and arrest deserters and to curtail those crossing over the mountains to join the Union army. Local families with men in Confederate service typically had few problems with the Home Guard. Those with men at home without leave or men who were trying to avoid service in either army learned that the Home Guard could be their worst enemy. At least 106 Toe River Valley men

John W. McElroy commanded the Yancey County militia and, later, the First Brigade North Carolina Home Guard. *State Archives of North Carolina.*

crossed over the mountains in 1863 to join the Federal army.[57]

Men went to great lengths to hide from both armies. Harmon Cox hid in the Burnt Mountain area, sleeping in barns in bad weather. Cox hoed corn for local families in exchange for food. Many trying to avoid service in both armies hid out at the Simerly Clearing near the head of Tom Creek in the Buladean area. Others hid in David Greer's Cave on Bald Mountain or in the massive hollow poplar tree that gave the Poplar community its name. When the conscription officers came for Thaddeus Braswell, he convinced them to allow him to gather wood for his family first. Every time he went out, he stayed a little longer, eventually disappearing into a rhododendron thicket. He spent more than three years living in a cave on Sugar Mountain. Occasionally, the Home Guard or other forces sent into the area captured someone. Leander Pyatt was hiding in the woods near his home. One evening, as he slipped in to repair the shoes of his children, he was caught by the Home Guard and dragged away while his children watched. Pyatt was assigned to the 58th North Carolina Troops but only lived a few weeks, dying in an Atlanta hospital. The Pyatt(e) community in Avery County is named for this family.[58]

Burnsville Raid

Conditions in the Toe River Valley continued to deteriorate. In April 1864, a group of forty women, dissatisfied with the aid provided by the state for the care of Confederate soldiers' widows and children, raided commissary stores in Burnsville. Whether orchestrated or by happenstance, a group of men arrived the next day. Led by Confederate deserter Montraville Ray, these dissidents stormed into town, shot the local conscription officer, broke into the local armory, stole five hundred pounds of bacon and then carried off the contents of a local store. They also assaulted Milton Penland, stealing food. "The county is gone up," John W. McElroy wrote two days later to Governor Vance from his headquarters at Mars Hill. Word arrived in

Asheville, and Colonel Palmer, now in charge of the Department of Western North Carolina, set out with a small force. A week after the raid, Palmer arrived and placed a cannon on a hill overlooking the town. After a few shells were lobbed into the center of town, Palmer ordered his men to charge, and the dissidents were chased out. The McElroy House was supposedly used as a field hospital. In retaliation for the destruction caused by the dissidents, Palmer ordered the store of Amos Ray burned. While many want to cast the combatants in the Burnsville Raid as "Blue" versus "Gray," there is nothing to indicate that Ray or the others were Unionists.[59]

Camp Vance Raid

In May 1864, several campaigns were launched across the South simultaneously in Virginia and Georgia to prevent Confederate forces in different states from reinforcing one another. Part of this plan involved destroying the bridge over the Yadkin River, severing one of two railroads connecting the Deep South with the Upper South. Chosen to lead this raid was Captain George W. Kirk, an East Tennessee Unionist who had spent most of the war recruiting men for Federal service. The raiders set out in June from Knoxville, heading to the terminus of the Western North Carolina railroad located near Camp Vance, Burke County. The nearly 125 men under Kirk's command included some soldiers and Cherokee Indians, but others were simply looking for opportunities to rob local citizens. After passing through Yellow Mountain Gap and working their way down Roaring Creek, the raiders, using local guides, worked their way down the North Toe River. After crossing the Linville River near Pineola, they spent an entire day and night working their way down the mountain. On the morning of June 28, they surrounded and captured the camp. Among those captured were 240 junior reserves, those not yet eighteen years old who were in the process of being organized into companies, thanks to an amended conscription law. Kirk burned the camp buildings, crossed back over the Catawba River and went into camp. His men commenced robbing indiscriminately. Several times throughout the following day, as Kirk's men worked their way back up the Winding Stairs Road, Home Guard and Confederate forces skirmished with Kirk's men. In one of those skirmishes, Kirk used his prisoners as human shields, laughing when they were shot. In another skirmish, W.W. Avery was mortally wounded, and Kirk was struck in the arm. That night, Kirk's men and prisoners camped in the Crossnore community. Two brothers who

George W. Kirk (*right*)—pictured with his father, Alexander (*standing*), and his brother, John (*left*)—led many raids into the Toe River Valley. *Matt Bumgarner.*

had been sprung from the Camp Vance stockade, Doran and Drury Clark, volunteered to go and burn Colonel Palmer's house in the present-day Altamont area. On July 9, Kirk, with prisoners in tow, arrived in Knoxville to a hero's welcome. Yet Kirk had failed in his mission to destroy the bridge over the Yadkin River.[60]

BATTLE OF BEECH MOUNTAIN

The Crab Orchard section of Carter County, Tennessee, was a haven for dissidents and bushwhackers who frequently slipped across the state line to raid farms for food and items, like livestock, that could be sold back in Tennessee. One such incursion took place in the fall of 1864, raiding though the Beverdams community in Watauga County and then passing back through Banner Elk before returning to Tennessee. Major Harvey Bingham, 11th Battalion North Carolina Home Guard, set out with a small group of soldiers to recover some of the stolen property. They recovered much of the livestock and captured several men in the Heaton, Dark Ridge and Poga areas before going into camp near Balm, all in present-day Avery County. The following day, the Home Guard was ambushed by Jim Hartley and a group of fifteen men. The Battle of Beech Mountain, which took place on the Avery-Watauga county line near the Matney Community, resulted in death for two members of the Home Guard: Dick Kilby and Elliott Bingham. After a few minutes of fighting, Hartley's group slipped back into the woods.[61]

DEATH OF JACKSON STEWART

There were many small altercations throughout the Toe River Valley. Homes were plundered and, at times, burned, and people were killed. Despite the presence of county sheriffs, the militia and the Home Guard, lawlessness abounded. Groups of deserters and dissidents used the mountains to hide. Certain areas—like "the land of Goshen" near Banner Elk, the Buladean area and "Taylor's Gut," near Roan Mountain—were frequent havens for these groups. Banner Elk served as a staging area for those seeking passage to Federal lines in East Tennessee. Once several men had gathered, a guide, such as Jim Hartley or William "Keese" Blalock, led them through the mountains into Kentucky and later to Knoxville. While some of these

Dan Ellis piloted dissidents and escaped Federal POWs through the mountains. *From* The Thrilling Adventures of Daniel Ellis *(1867)*.

groups were aided by locals, many stole food and clothing to survive the mountain trek. Several times, regular Confederate soldiers were sent into the region to break up these bands of bushwhackers.[62]

Some forays produced retaliatory raids across the state lines. In November 1864, a group of "East Tennessee tories" raided into the Bakersville area. Sixteen local men were captured. Robert Penland was beaten, Jackson Stewart was killed and "much property was destroyed and carried off," including up to thirty horses and numerous cattle. The story of the death of Stewart later grew, though never like those about his sister, Frankie Silver, hanged thirty years earlier. He was responsible for collecting taxes and went to seize several horses from Unionists for nonpayment. After taking the horses, he was ambushed and shot several times. In one account, the Unionists cut off his head and placed it on a pole before riding back into Bakersville.[63]

Toward the end of 1864, the trickle of men crossing over the mountain to join the Federal army turned into a stream. In 1864, 162 men made this trek, while another 56 men joined a Federal regiment in the last few weeks of the war. Those men who crossed over the mountains in 1862 and 1863 typically joined the 8th Tennessee or 13th Tennessee Cavalry (U.S.). The majority who waited until the last few months of the war frequently enlisted in the 3rd North Carolina Mounted Infantry (U.S.). Unfortunately, the men who joined

Members of the Colonel John B. Palmer Camp Sons of Confederate Veterans dedicated the Mitchell County Confederate Memorial in 2011. *Author's collection.*

this regiment did most of the raiding on their neighbors' farms in the Toe River Valley. One historian labeled the 3rd North Carolina as "a notorious band of scoundrels and thieves." Judging from the 1860 census, 1,209 Toe River valley men joined the Confederate army, while 337 joined the Federal army. Of those 337 Federal soldiers, 157 were Confederate deserters. Those who died in battle, from wounds or of disease numbered 236 Confederates and 41 Federals. The actual numbers are undoubtedly higher, as the 1860 census missed scores of families. Seldom discussed are the hundreds of men of military age who simply avoided the war at all costs.[64]

The Toe River Valley was irrevocably changed by the events of the 1860s, as evidenced by cemeteries across the three counties. Tombstones, often provided by the Veterans Administration, dot the area's graveyards. Both sides, often members of the same family, are frequently represented in the same cemeteries. There was discussion of organizing a Grand Army of the Republic in Cranberry in 1887, but no evidence exists that those efforts were successful. The General Pender Camp 1154, United Confederate Veterans, was established in Burnsville in about 1900 and existed for a number of years. Since 2001, the Colonel John B. Palmer Camp 1946, Sons of Confederate Veterans, has labored to mark graves, erect monuments and educate the public about the role the Toe River Valley played in the complex history of the American Civil War.[65]

Chapter 10

BLUE RIDGE PARKWAY

History Hidden in Plain Sight

It probably comes as no surprise that the Blue Ridge Parkway is the most visited park within the National Park System, drawing almost 16 million visitors in 2021. The parkway begins at Mile Marker 0 in Virginia and ends in North Carolina at Mile Marker 469, connecting the Shenandoah National Park with the Great Smoky Mountains National Park. Fifty-seven miles of the beautiful roadway skirt the southern edge of the Toe River Valley. Many of the parkway's most popular areas—such as Linville Falls, Beacon Heights, Chestoa View and Crabtree Falls, plus Mount Mitchell State Park—are all accessed from this segment.

Before the Blue Ridge Parkway came the Crest of the Blue Ridge Highway. Traces of this road can still be found hidden along sections of the current parkway in Mitchell County. Behind this scenic road was Joseph J. Pratt, head of the North Carolina Geological and Economic Survey. The year was 1909, and Pratt envisioned a 350-mile road from Marion, Virginia, to Tallulah Falls, Georgia, with Toe River Valley sections passing through Linville, Pineola, Altapass and Little Switzerland. Surveying was completed by 1911, and construction began soon thereafter. The road was twenty-four feet wide, with a sand-clay or gravel surface, and portions between Pineola and Altapass were completed before World War I ended construction.

The idea of the current scenic road through the Blue Ridge Mountains was born amid the Great Depression. Senator Harry F. Byrd of Virginia and President Franklin D. Roosevelt both claimed credit for the concept. In June 1933, the Blue Ridge Parkway was authorized by the National

Recovery Act. In May 1934, the group responsible for surveying the route was traveling "through the picturesque Mayland area of Western North Carolina." By early 1936, survey maps had been completed. Much of the BRP passed through the Pisgah National Forest, land already owned by the federal government. However, some sections of the surveyed route passed through privately owned property. These survey maps were signed by the local register of deeds and posted in local courthouses. People could see the maps to learn if their property had been seized for the construction of the road. Although compensated, R.S. Belleu, Clyde Bailey, Glenn Mashburn and J.A. Bowditch all had portions of their property taken. Construction on the local section began in July 1936, and it was estimated to be halfway completed by the following January. This section of the BRP required several tunnels to be cut through the mountains, including the Little Switzerland Tunnel, Wildacres Tunnel, Twin Tunnels (although one is one hundred feet longer than the other) and Rough Ridge Tunnel. Portions of the road between Buck Creek Gap and Big Laurel Mountain in Yancey County were expected to be completed in the summer of 1937. Work on the section

A property dispute delayed completion of the Blue Ridge Parkway around Grandfather Mountain until the 1980s. *Blue Ridge Parkway.*

between Grandfather Mountain and Linville Falls did not commence until 1938. With the entry of the United States into World War II, work on the BRP came to a halt. The section beyond Black Mountain Gap did not open to the public until August 1950.[66]

Every mile along the Blue Ridge Parkway is indicated with a mile post marker. There is quite a bit of hidden history in the Avery-Mitchell-Yancey County segments. At Mile Marker 304 is the Linn Cove Viaduct, the last section of the Blue Ridge Parkway, completed in 1987. The "missing link" was delayed for years as the National Park Service and Hugh Morton, owner of Grandfather Mountain, debated the route. The NPS wanted a higher route, while Morton wanted a lower route. They finally agreed on a middle approach, and the 1,243-foot-long bridge spanned the Linn Cove boulder field. There is a hiking trail and seasonally opened visitor's center.

Brown Mountain can be viewed from the Lost Cove Cliffs Parking area at Mile Marker 310. The famous Brown Mountain Lights are recorded in both song and story. One legend states that the mysterious lights are torches carried by maidens looking for loved ones after the Cherokees and Catawbas fought a pitched battle along the slopes.[67]

North Carolina Highway 181 crosses the BRP at Mile Marker 312. Parts of this road are called Winding Stairs, an old road leading down the mountain to Morganton. Federal raiders crossed through this gap in June 1864 en route to attack Camp Vance and fought several skirmishes with local Home Guard forces as they returned across the mountains with prisoners and plunder.

Linville Falls, at Mile Marker 316, is one of the most visited areas on the BRP, featuring a campground, picnic area and numerous hiking trails traveling above and to the pool of the falls. The area was a camp for Confederates processing iron ore during the Civil War, a tourist camp in the early 1900s and a gristmill. The property was purchased by John D. Rockefeller Jr. to be preserved as part of the Blue Ridge Parkway.

McKinney Gap is named for the family of Charles McKinney, believed to have had four wives and forty-eight children, all at once. He is buried nearby. Mile Marker 327 passes through McKinney Gap.

Mile Marker 328 has an overlook for the Loops. This section of the old Carolina, Clinchfield and Ohio Railroad is twenty-nine miles long, containing eighteen tunnels and descending 1,350 feet. The railroad, now operated by CSX, passes under the parkway near here.

Gillespie Gap is where the Blue Ridge Parkway crosses NC226A. Both Little Switzerland and Spruce Pine can be accessed here. Mile Marker

The only three-arch bridge on the entire Blue Ridge Parkway passes over the Linville River. *Author's collection.*

330 is also the location of the Museum of North Carolina Minerals. Gillespie Gap is named for Henry Gillespie. A Tory living in Turkey Cove in present-day McDowell County, Gillespie was dragged out of bed in September 1780 by the Overmountain Men, who were attempting to gain information regarding the movements of Ferguson's Loyalists. The route of the Overmountain Men passed through the gap, one of the major entries into the Toe River Valley.

Lynn Gap, at Mile Marker 332, is named for a large basswood (or Lynn) tree that once stood on the Mitchell-McDowell county line. Also known as the Marrying Tree, a landmark where local couples met just over the line to wed, the tree was cut down in 1965.

Wildacres Tunnel is named for the nearby Wildacres Retreat center, started by Thomas Dixon in the 1920s, and is at Mile Marker 336.

Behind Linville Falls as the most visited waterfall on the Parkway is Crabtree Falls, located at Mile Marker 339 and originally called Murphy Falls before being renamed by the National Park Service in the 1940s. It's considered one of the top ten most photogenic waterfalls in North Carolina. The name for the falls and area comes from several crabapple orchards nearby. Also nearby were feldspar mines active in the 1920s.[68]

The Big Lynn Tree was a well-known landmark in Little Switzerland. *State Archives of North Carolina.*

Buck Creek Gap, at Mile Marker 244, is one of the few gaps through the Blue Ridge allowing entry to the Toe River Valley.

At Mile Marker 355 is Black Mountain Gap and access to Mount Mitchell State Park via NC 128. Originally called Swannanoa Gap, its name was changed in 1949 to avoid confusion with the other Swannanoa Gap on the Buncombe-McDowell county line.[69]

Top: Guests enjoyed a visitor's center, gift shop and restaurant at Crabtree Meadows in 1974. *Blue Ridge Parkway Historic Photograph Collection.*

Bottom: The Blue Ridge Parkway travels over Highway 80 at Buck Creek Gap, circa 1944. *State Archives of North Carolina.*

The Blue Ridge Parkway hugs the Yancey County line, dipping more often into Buncombe County, but for a brief moment, it ducks back into Yancey County near Walker Knob Overlook, Mile Marker 359. Earlier, this spot was known as the Balsam Gap parking area, providing access to the Big Butt Trail.

For many people, the Blue Ridge Parkway is an excellent introduction to the wonders of the Toe River Valley, including some often-hidden features.

Chapter 11

THE LOST RAILROADS OF THE TOE RIVER VALLEY

One hundred years ago, the lonesome wail of a steam engine's whistle could be heard across the Toe River Valley. In the early twenty-first century, even the low rumble of a diesel locomotive winding its way down the steep mountains is a rare sound. More than a score of railroads have history hidden in the Toe River Valley. A few became reality, while most only existed on paper. Railroads were vital to the growth of a town or community. They provided a way for farmers to get products to market. Mica, iron ore, feldspar and other minerals mined locally could be transported to factories, even when roads were few. Many railroads hauled out local timber used to support building booms, especially in the 1920s. People could order products via the mail, the items arriving via the railroad. Plus, if the rail company provided passenger service, people could get on the train and travel to nearly any place in the United States serviced by a railroad. Finally, the railroads themselves provided jobs for men working on track crews, cutting railroad ties, servicing the engines, shoveling coal and filling an array of positions in the various yards.

It took time to complete a railroad. As early as 1854, it was recognized that the Toe River Valley was "perhaps more disadvantageously situated than any of the" other counties in the state. In August 1855, at a railroad meeting in Burnsville, local people voted to send delegates to Morganton for an upcoming "Railroad Convention." Even a railroad in neighboring Burke County would affect the Toe River Valley. However, it was only after the Civil War that the discussion regarding railroads became serious.[70]

THE EAST TENNESSEE AND WESTERN NORTH CAROLINA RAILROAD (ET&WNC)

In 1866, the Tennessee General Assembly passed legislation incorporating the East Tennessee and Western North Carolina Railroad to run from Johnson City through Elizabethton, Doe River and Crab Orchard on to the Tennessee line. The Cranberry Iron Works, not far away, was the final destination. Construction did not begin until June 1868, and five miles of track had been laid by April 1870. However, poor financial decisions forced the sale of the company in November 1871. The line was sold again in 1873, and in 1879, a decision was made to rebuild the railroad as a narrow-gauge line. Construction began in September 1880. The most direct route took the line through the Doe River Gorge. Several tunnels were excavated, and a roadbed was constructed on the side of a mountain overlooking the gorge. By June 1882, the track had reached Cranberry. Regular passenger and freight service began on July 3, 1882. The primary purpose of the ET&WNC was to haul out iron ore from the mines at Cranberry. Everything

An early ET&WNC Railroad engine stops at the Cranberry Depot. *University of North Carolina–Chapel Hill, Wilson Library Special Collections.*

The ET&WNC passed through Elk Park, pictured here, before terminating in Cranberry. *Avery County Historical Museum.*

else that traveled on the railway—including lumber, passengers and other freight—was secondary.[71]

Depots were constructed in Elk Park and Cranberry. Elk Park was born as the railroad approached. The post office in Elk Park was established in 1883. Soon, Elk Park became a shipping point for people living in Mitchell and Watauga Counties. Local residents constructed the Valle Crucis, Shawneehaw and Elk Park Turnpike, a sixteen-mile toll road connecting the railroad with the Valle Crucis community. "We will bring our country within the bounds of civilized man," one local wrote. With the railroad and new roads, Elk Park became a thriving community. Cranberry had a post office for decades prior to the arrival of the railroad. The railroad brought a depot, the Cranberry Inn, a swimming pool, a baseball field and a union church.[72]

Several factors hurt the ET&WNC. The Cranberry mines closed in 1929. While there was talk of reopening, that never happened. The timber industry was also played out by the 1930s. When the flood of 1940 damaged the Linville River Railway, south of Cranberry, the LRR was abandoned. The ET&WNC survived for another decade and, during the World War II years, hauled people to war-related jobs in Elizabethton. On October 16, 1950, the ET&WNC made the last run to Elk Park and Cranberry. Then the rails were removed and the depots were torn down. The shrill pitch of "Tweetsie" would not be heard again in the Toe River Valley.[73]

LINVILLE RIVER RAILWAY (LRR)

Almost as soon as the ET&WNC was finished, different enterprising individuals wanted to attach a new railroad to the terminus at Cranberry. There was talk of expanding the Carolina Central Railway through the mountains. The Southern and Western Air Line, connecting Shelby, North Carolina, to Cranberry via Linville, was proposed in 1889, and the Cranberry and Linville Railroad was planned in 1890. In July 1896, the North Carolina General Assembly granted a charter to the Linville River Railroad. The largest shareholders, the Camp brothers from Chicago, had recently purchased a small sawmill in Saginaw, planning to enlarge the operation. Surveying and much of the grading from Cranberry to Saginaw (Pineola) was completed by the spring of 1897. The line was frequently referred to as the "Arbuckle Coffee Line" for the Arbuckle Coffee labels sent in exchange for merchandise through the company's popular promotion.[74]

By late 1897, the Camp brothers had exhausted their funding, and the proposed line was auctioned. William Ritter purchased the railroad and, in April 1899, began laying track to Pineola for the recently incorporated Linville River Railway. One newspaper referred to this line as the Cranberry and Pineola Railroad. Like the ET&WNC, the LRR was a narrow-gauge line. The smaller engines, Shays and Climaxes, were better equipped to handle the tight turns and steep grades of the mountains. Ritter exhausted his timber rights in the area by 1913, when he moved his operation to Caldwell County. He placed the LRR up for sale. It was purchased by the East Tennessee Coal and Coke Company, which also owned the ET&WNC.[75]

From Cranberry, the LRR moved south through Cranberry Gap to Minneapolis before turning east toward Newland, passing through the communities of Ivy Heights, Buchanan and Vale. For much of the route between Minneapolis and Newland, the railroad ran parallel to the North Toe River and, in three different instances, bridged the river. From Newland, the LRR followed Kentucky Creek to Montezuma and then turned toward Pineola. Numerous spurs were constructed at Pineola, temporary lines into the virgin stands of timber. Once the timber was harvested, the rails were taken up and reused to reach another stand. Another timber baron, William Whiting, stepped into the picture in 1913, purchasing timber rights in the Shulls Mill area of Watauga County. Whiting asked that the LRR be extended to Shulls Mill so that the lumber could be taken to market.

The LRR depot, *left*, once sat at the heart of the Montezuma community. *Avery County Historical Museum.*

The plan was approved in July 1915, and by September 1916, the rails had reached the Boone Fork Lumber Company in Shulls Mill. Shortly thereafter, the line reached Boone. Minneapolis, Buchanan, Vale, Linville Gap, Jestes Siding and Townsend were flag stops with simple shelters, while Newland, Montezuma, Pineola and Linville had depots. At 4,012 feet above sea level, the flag stop in Linville Gap was the highest point served by a passenger train in the eastern United States.[76]

Freshets, or floods, have always been a problem in the mountains. Major storms, including hurricanes, stall over the mountains, dumping copious amounts of rain and pushing streams and creeks out of their banks. Serious floods occurred in 1901 and 1916, yet the railroads were rebuilt. Then fifteen inches of rain fell on August 13, 1940, destroying homes and businesses. The North Toe River overflowed between Minneapolis and Newland, taking out bridges and fills, while the swollen Linville River destroyed portions of the track near the town of Linville. Since there had been a steady decline of business for the railroad, the parent company chose to apply for abandonment instead of rebuilding. While many local people fought hard to keep the railroad, the Interstate Commerce Committee agreed with the company's petition, and in November 1940, the LRR was abandoned. The surviving rails and boxcars were loaded on trucks and shipped out of the area, while depots were sold as surplus to local citizens. Portions of the old train bed can still be found hidden in the woods. However, the LRR is just a fading memory.

MARION AND CRANBERRY RAILROAD (M&C)

There seem to have been several attempts to build the Marion and Cranberry Railroad. A request for a charter was introduced into the General Assembly in 1871. However, the bill to establish this line was defeated. In 1881, there was a mention of a meeting regarding a railroad that would stretch from Spartanburg, South Carolina, through Rutherfordton and Marion to the Cranberry Iron Works. Talk of this line continued through 1885. The proposed railroad appears to have become the Carolina, Clinchfield and Ohio, which bypasses Cranberry in favor of Spruce Pine. A final mention of the original project was in 1888 with the Shelby, Marion and Cranberry Railroad.[77]

MARION AND NORTHWESTERN RAILROAD (M&N)

Chartered in 1901, the proposed Marion and Northwestern Railroad line would "traverse a section of the state rich in mineral deposits and covered with fine timber." The M&N was thirty-one miles in length, connecting Marion with the line in Huntdale. Stockholders included not only North Carolinians, like Julian S. Carr, but also men from Richmond, Philadelphia and Boston.[78]

Marion, Linville and Cranberry Railway

The charter of the proposed Marion, Linville and Cranberry Railway line was repealed in February 1905, making it yet another Toe River Valley railway that only ever existed on paper and in the failed plans of those who envisioned it.[79]

Atlanta, Asheville and Baltimore Railroad (AA&B)

The proposed Atlanta, Asheville and Baltimore Railroad line was planned to run through the mountain counties from Asheville. Local residents met in December 1887 to consider voting on subscribing $50,000 in capital stock to ensure that the line traveled through the Toe River Valley. Subscriptions for the line began in 1889. However, discussion of this line disappears from the public record soon thereafter.[80]

Asheville and Burnsville Railroad (A&B)

Incorporated in 1883, the Asheville and Burnsville Railroad Company was led by Robert B. Vance, congressman and former Confederate general. Vance had ties to the Toe River Valley. There was quite a bit of wrangling over the route of the line. A survey of a route connecting with the ET&WNC at Cranberry proved too expensive. Another proposal was to connect a line to Embreeville, Carter County, and thence to Jonesborough. By the end of the year, coverage of the A&B proposed route had disappeared from local newspapers.[81]

Asheville and Burnsville Railroad (A&B)

The idea of a railroad connecting Asheville and Burnsville came up again in 1905 when the Asheville and Burnsville was again chartered. The proposed new line would connect with the CC&O at Boonford, pass through Burnsville and then travel on to Asheville. However, at a meeting in Burnsville in August, citizens voted down the issuance of $50,000 in bonds to help facilitate the building of the A&B.[82]

SOUTHERN AND WESTERN AIR LINE RAILROAD (S&WAL)

As planned, the Southern and Western Air Line would connect Cranberry with Morganton, and overall, it would travel from the Virginia state line to the South Carolina line. This railroad was chartered in February 1885. Surveying work began on the section between Shelby and Morganton in April 1887, but it never proceeded farther north. By late 1887, the line was in legal trouble. The line was built in other places, but it never reached the Toe River Valley.[83]

CRANBERRY AND LINVILLE RAILROAD (C&L)

The Cranberry and Linville first appeared in local newspapers in November 1896. It can be assumed that the line stretched from the terminus of the ET&WNC in Cranberry all the way to the lumberyard in Linville. There were hopes that the line would continue on to the John's River area of Caldwell County. If this line was ever surveyed or if any grading work was started, documentation appears lost to history.[84]

MICA BELT RAILROAD (MBR)

In September 1910, the Mica Belt Railroad was front-page news in Asheville, having just received its charter. The proposed fifteen-mile line was to run from Cranberry to Minneapolis, down the North Toe River to Plumtree and "thence to some point on the Carolina, Clinchfield & Ohio railroad between Alta Pass and Spruce Pine." Behind this railroad effort were T.B. Vance, T.D. Vance, R.M. Burleson, Frank Burleson, Sam Burleson and Ira Vance. It is possible that parts of this proposed line were completed between Alta Pass and the Loops by the Meadows Company of Bristol, Tennessee. It was a lumber line and might have been known locally as the "Humpback Mountain Line."[85]

BRISTOL AND ASHEVILLE RAILROAD (B&A)

The planned Bristol and Asheville Railroad line was to extend from Elizabethton, Tennessee, via one of two proposed routes. The first would have moved up Little Doe River and McKinney Creek to a gap in Iron Mountain. The other was proposed through Gap Creek, down Sciota Creek, up Indian Creek and through a gap in the Iron Mountains. After crossing into North Carolina, the railroad followed Spring Creek to Big Rock Creek and then into the Toe River Valley. Following the river, it entered Yancey County, up Jack's Creek, "across a low divide; thence to Caney River," where it entered into Madison County near Paint Gap.[86]

CAROLINA, CLINCHFIELD AND OHIO RAILROAD (CC&O)

There was much discussion through the nineteenth century of a railroad linking Charleston, South Carolina, with the coalfields of eastern Kentucky and the great Ohio River Valley area. Numerous routes were proposed, such as the Louisville, Cincinnati and Charleston Railroad in 1831 and the Blue Ridge Railroad in 1851. Most took the railroad through Asheville and along the French Broad. The Civil War brought any construction to a halt and impoverished the South.

In September 1886, John Wilder, owner of the Cloudland Hotel with interests in various local iron ore mines, received a charter for the Charleston, Cincinnati and Chicago Railroad, a 625-mile railroad connecting rich agricultural lands and coal fields of central Appalachia with the Atlantic coast. Work grading and surveying various portions of the line began in several places. Citizens of Yancey County, in 1889, sought to divert the line from Mitchell into Yancey. However, the Panic of 1893 halted construction. The line was purchased and renamed the Ohio River and Charleston Railroad. Construction resumed, and after navigating the Nolichucky Gorge, the line reached Huntdale in 1899 and Boonford in 1902. The line was sold in 1902 to George L. Carter. Construction continued, this time under the name of the South and Western Railway. In 1905, the line moved south of Spruce Pine, reaching Altapass that October. Numerous tunnels were constructed below Altapass. Camps were established for up to four thousand laborers brought to tunnel through the mountains. A narrow-gauge line was constructed from Altapass to Washburn Ridge to funnel supplies. The Vance Tunnel was constructed in Altapass, and the Blue Ridge Tunnel took the line into McDowell County. Construction was completed on this section of the line in 1908.[87]

The workers brought in to help blast out the mountainsides were mostly Italians fleeing rural poverty in southern Italy and Sicily. Many found

Train tracks run through the gorge of the Nolichucky in a Paul M. Fink photograph, circa 1920. *Southern Appalachian Digital Collection, Western Carolina University.*

The old Clinchfield Railroad passed through fifty-four tunnels, including Vance Tunnel in Mitchell County. *John L. Burns.*

Awaiting the train at the Spruce Pine depot, 1943, was a familiar scene in many Toe River Valley communities. *State Archives of North Carolina.*

work in mining camps and construction projects. Others were African Americans, Germans and a few Russians. Violence erupted in the camps from time to time.

On March 31, 1908, a new charter was granted. The line was now called the Carolina, Clinchfield and Ohio Railroad. The line ran from Elkhorn City, Kentucky, to Spartanburg, South Carolina, with headquarters in Erwin, Tennessee. The final line was 277 miles long. Passenger service between Johnson City and Marion began in September. Eventually, there were stops at Lost Cove, Narrows, Poplar, Peterson, Huntdale, Relief, Green Mountain, Forbes, Toecane, Galax, Boonford, Phillips, Penland and Spruce Pine.[88]

In 1924, the Atlantic Coast Line agreed to lease the CC&O for ninety-nine years, and the line became known simply as the Clinchfield Railroad. Coal was always the mainstay of the line, although other freight and passenger service continued. Passenger service was finally discontinued in 1954. In the 1970s, the familiar Clinchfield logo disappeared and was replaced with the Family Lines System emblem. Then it transformed into the Seaboard System, the Chessie System and, later, to CSX.

Caney River Railroad (CRR)

An act to incorporate the Caney River Railroad was introduced into the General Assembly in 1903. The plan of this line was an eighteen-mile road from Huntdale to Bald Mountain, where the Bald Mountain Lumber Company was located, in Yancey County. At Huntdale, it connected to the South and Western Railroad. There was also the possibility that the line would stretch all the way to Burnsville. David Buck was president of the line. In 1904, the narrow-gauge CRR had three Climax engines, twenty-two cars and one coach. The line was sold to Doss Lumber Company in 1912, which continued to log until 1925, when the operation was closed.[89]

Black Mountain Railroad (BMR)

Begun in 1907, the Black Mountain Railroad was a standard-gauge, eight-mile line that connected the South and Western Railroad in Kona to Bowditch. A large lumber mill was set up there to process the timber on the twelve-thousand-acre property formerly owned by the Murchison Lumber

Company. From Micaville, the line extended to Burnsville in 1912 and, in 1913, to Athlone. Many hoped that the BMR would eventually connect to Asheville. Other spurs were built to access tracts of timber to the BMR. In 1913, ownership of the BMR passed to CC&O, which continued to operate the line until 1951. The BMR applied for abandonment through the Interstate Commerce Commission; this was granted in 1954, with the provision that the railroad would be put up for sale. Local citizens bought the line and renamed it the Yancey Railroad. The BMR's biggest client was the Feldspar Corporation, which closed the plant in Bowditch in 1971. The line held on until 1984, and in 1985, the remaining assets were auctioned off. Technically, the Yancey Railroad was never declared abandoned.[90]

AVERY AND NORTHWESTERN RAILROAD (A&N)

The Avery and Northwestern Railroad was incorporated in 1915 with plans to run from Edgemont in Caldwell County to Newland. Avery County was scheduled to vote for a $100,000 bond to help with construction. Potter Brown of Newland was listed as president of the A&N. The proposed line was to enter Avery County either at Ivy Gap, near Pineola, or above Linville on the Yonnahlossee Turnpike. The line would connect Johnson City with Hickory as a narrow-gauge railroad until enough businesses developed to support a standard-gauge line. Just why this line failed is unclear.[91]

CRABTREE CREEK RAILROAD (CCR)

Mitchell County's Crabtree Creek Railroad is a bit of a mystery. A 1935 U.S. Geological Survey map shows a dismantled railroad line that intersects the South and Western above Boonford. The line follows the county line between Yancey and Mitchell south. This is believed to be the Crabtree Creek Railroad, a narrow-gauge line that serviced Crabtree Feldspar Company located near Crabtree Falls. The location of where the CRR intersected the S&W was a flag stop known as Cass. This railroad existed sometime between 1921 and 1935.[92]

SANFORD AND TREADWAY RAILROAD

Sanford and Treadway began purchasing timber rights in Avery County near Cranberry and Newland in 1913. The company had been cutting timber in neighboring Carter County for at least a decade. One historian contends that Sanford and Treadway built a lumberyard where Newland currently sits and laid rails to Cranberry. This line was later acquired by W.M. Ritter and became the Linville River Railway. It is also believed that some of the rolling stock was acquired by the D&H Lumber Company, which ran out of Linville and cut timber on Grandfather Mountain.[93]

"HOOT OWL RAILROAD"

The Dibell Mineral Company operated several feldspar mines in Mitchell County, including the Hoot Owl Mine near Penland. Around 1919, the company built a line from its mine to Penland, connecting to the CC&O. Small loads of feldspar were transported to regular cars using side dump ore cars. The line was apparently not in use by 1930. Since the mine was the Hoot Owl Mine, the small railroad was known as the "Hoot Owl Railroad."[94]

Chapter 12

A FEW PLACE NAMES
WITH HIDDEN HISTORY

T he names of communities, towns and geographical features in the Toe River Valley often contain hidden history. Some of the stories remain, perhaps mixed with a helping of folklore.

ALTAPASS (MITCHELL COUNTY). Named by the Clinchfield Railroad in the early 1900s, "Alta" means high elevation, while "pass" refers to the nearby McKinney Gap. Altapass was the highest depot on the Clinchfield line. The community once boasted the Holman Hospital and Holman Public Library. The library was destroyed by an arsonist in June 1930.[95]

BAKERSVILLE (MITCHELL COUNTY). The county seat of Mitchell County was known as Baker's Place, or Baker's Plantation, after Revolutionary War veteran and early settler David Baker. The earliest mention of Bakersville in a newspaper is in 1830.[96]

BANDANA (MITCHELL COUNTY). A Clinchfield Railroad depot was planned in an area where there were frequent stops, so to mark the location, a brakeman hung a bandana on a laurel bush.[97]

BANNER ELK (AVERY COUNTY). Originally known as "Hix Settlement" or the "Larkin Chopping," the community became Banner's Elk in 1848 when the Banner family arrived, and it became a stop on a local "underground railroad" funneling escaped Federal prisoners and dissidents to Kentucky and Tennessee during the Civil War. Originally incorporated as Shawneehaw in 1891, it was reincorporated in 1911 as Banner's Elk. The post office was established on June 16, 1875.[98]

Altapass once boasted a hotel, hospital and library due to the railroad. *University of North Carolina–Chapel Hill, Wilson Library Special Collections.*

The second Mitchell County Courthouse occupies the center of this 1895 Bakersville image. *Dan Barron.*

BLACK MOUNTAINS (YANCEY COUNTY). This range of mountains takes its name from the dark evergreen spruce and fir trees on the slopes.[99]

BOONFORD (MITCHELL COUNTY). It is rumored that Daniel Boone once forded the North Toe River at this spot. Another story is that the community is named for Robert Boone, a local Confederate soldier. A convict camp was located nearby in the early twentieth century.[100]

BULADEAN (MITCHELL COUNTY). Original names for this community include Magnetic City and Wilder's Forge. Wilder was also the owner of Cloudland Hotel. The post office was established as Wilders in 1881, changed to Magnetic City in 1887 and changed again in 1918 to Buladean. It was discontinued in 1955.[101]

BURNSVILLE (YANCEY COUNTY). Established as the county seat of Yancey County in 1834, Burnsville was named for War of 1812 naval hero Captain Otway Burns, who has a monument in town but is buried in Beaufort, Carteret County. The town of Otway in Carteret County is also named for him.

CELO (YANCEY COUNTY). The name is possibly a corruption of Selu, the Cherokees' first woman and wife of Kana'ti.[102]

CLARISSA (MITCHELL COUNTY). Named after early settler Clarissa Baker Buchanan, the town of Clarissa had a post office established in 1897, discontinued in 1952.[103]

Burnsville's Otway Burns statue looks west toward the third courthouse (*left*) and the old bank (*right*). *Author's collection.*

Stores, the public school, the hospital and the Baptist church, hidden in the trees, *left*, were centerpieces of the Crossnore community. *Clark family.*

CRANBERRY (AVERY COUNTY). The area was originally called Cranberry Forge, due to the wild cranberries and the iron forge.

CROSSNORE (AVERY COUNTY). George Crossnore, who took large land grants in the area in the 1790s, is the town's namesake. It is believed that he operated a small store where the town hall is currently located.[104]

DOBAG CREEK (YANCEY COUNTY). A man, carrying a bag of meal home and being a little tipsy, stumbled and dropped his meal in the creek. He retrieved his bag and, upon reaching home, found his meal in a doughy state. Hence, the name of "Doughbag" Creek was created. There was a community of Dobag with a post office established in 1881 and discontinued in 1907.[105]

ELK PARK (AVERY COUNTY). Named for the elk that once roamed the area and for a portion of Hump Mountain that resembled a park, Elk Park was constructed about a mile north of the Cranberry mines. While Cranberry was a company town with company-owned business, anyone could open a business in Elk Park. After the formation of Avery County in 1911, Elk Park served as the county seat while Newland was being built.[106]

EGYPT (YANCEY COUNTY). One possible explanation is that after a year with no summer, maybe 1816, the area that became Egypt was the only area not affected by a summer freeze. Folks came from all over to acquire seeds for planting. Egypt refers to the Bible story about Egypt avoiding famine and feeding others, under the leadership of Joseph, who had interpreted the prophetic dreams of the pharaoh.[107]

GEORGE'S FORK (YANCEY COUNTY). Cooney George was once out hunting and fell between the prongs or forks of a large dogwood tree. He was unable to extract himself and had to call for help until he was rescued.[108]

HUNTDALE (MITCHELL COUNTY). According to a local story, a man had a wife named Dale who frequently ran off, and her husband would come looking for her. He was out hunting for Dale—hence, Huntdale.[109]

INGALLS (AVERY COUNTY). The community was named in honor of U.S. Senator James J. Ingalls. Representing Kansas from 1872 until 1891, Ingalls was a proposed presidential candidate who advocated for women's suffrage and African American civil rights.[110]

JACK'S CREEK (YANCEY COUNTY). Originally, this location was known as McDowell Creek, probably for the McDowell family of Burke County, who owned property in the area. Later, a bear-hunting dog named Jack cornered a bear at the creek.[111]

KONA (MITCHELL COUNTY). This name is a shortened version of the chemical makeup of feldspar: K for potassium, O for oxygen and Na for sodium.[112]

LEDGER (MITCHELL COUNTY). A man named Phillips submitted a report to the postal service in a ledger, and the postal service named the community after the ledger.[113]

Kona was once a thriving town with stores, churches and school. *John L. Burns.*

LICKSKILLET CREEK (YANCEY COUNTY). Near the end of the Civil War, a group of Federal raiders, possibly under the notorious George W. Kirk, ate all the food they could find, even licking the skillet clean.[114]

LINVILLE (AVERY COUNTY). There are many places in Avery County named for William Linville and his son, who, according to the traditional story, left the Yadkin River late in the summer of 1766, traveling west to hunt with John Williams. A party of Indians, possibly Shawnees, killed the two Linvilles. Williams survived to tell the story. A group, possibly including Daniel Boone, returned to the area, found the remains of the Linvilles and buried them.[115]

LITTLE SWITZERLAND (MITCHELL COUNTY). The community, which once had the Kilmichael Tower atop Grassy Ridge, was founded as a resort in 1910 by Charlotte judge and later associate justice of the North Carolina Supreme Court Heriot Clarkson. The resemblance to the mountains in Switzerland gave the area its name, and the town was famous for fighting against eminent domain seizure by the National Park Service.[116]

LOAFERS GLORY (MITCHELL COUNTY). In about 1890, Jonathan Burleson may have named this community after men who enjoyed "loafering" on the front porch of a local general store instead of working.[117]

LOST COVE (YANCEY COUNTY). According to local tradition, Lost Cove, above the Nolichucky River, was settled during or right after the Civil War. A wagon road was constructed in 1912, and due to the logging in the area (and the arrival of the railroad), the community prospered. Once the timber

The Little Switzerland community in lower Mitchell County included summer homes, primarily for Charlotte residents. *Author's collection.*

In Loafers Glory, local women frowned on "loafering" men. *Dan Barron.*

was all logged, the community began to fade. Local residents lobbied to have a road built into the community, but the General Assembly denied their request. The town was abandoned in 1957. What is left of the community is only accessible by hiking.[118]

MINNEAPOLIS (AVERY COUNTY). The post office here was established on June 30, 1892. The community was named in honor of Minneapolis, Minnesota, by Dr. L.E. Clark. The name comes from the Sioux word *minne* (water) and the Greek word *polis* (city).[119]

MINPRO (MITCHELL COUNTY). A workman at one of the many mineral processing plants in the area suggested the name, basing it on the mineral products.[120]

MONTEZUMA (AVERY COUNTY). Montezuma, the location of a salt lick, was once called Bull Scrape because of the large number of bulls scraping the ground with their hooves. In 1883, a post office was established and named Aaron, in honor of Aaron Franklin. In 1891, the town was incorporated and renamed Montezuma.[121]

NOLICHUCKY (MITCHELL COUNTY). The name evidently comes from the word *Nolichuckquah*, meaning "a spruce pine."[122]

PENLAND (MITCHELL COUNTY). Named for early settler and businessman Milton Penland; the post office was established in 1879.[123]

Left: A postcard commemorates the arrival of the first passenger train in the Pensacola community in Yancey County. *Yancey History Association*.

Below: The Plumtree community was originally settled by the Avery family. *Author's collection*.

Bird's-eye View of Plumtree, N. C.

PENSACOLA (YANCEY COUNTY). The name is possibly a Native American word for "forked valley."[124]

PLUMTREE (AVERY COUNTY). Settlers found hundreds of wild plum trees growing near the North Toe River. It was originally called Plumtree Orchards, Avery's Bottom or Avery's Quarters; the post office was established on February 23, 1874.[125]

POPLAR (MITCHELL COUNTY). According to local stories, a giant hollow poplar tree here once sheltered livestock and soldiers during the Civil War. The post office, Hollow Poplar, was established in 1872. The name was shortened to Poplar in 1896, and the post office was discontinued in 1959.[126]

Possum Trot Creek (Yancey County). Originally named McElroy Creek after the John W. McElroy family, the community was later renamed for the many possums.[127]

Red Hill (Mitchell County). After a large rain, all that was left on the ground was the red soil underneath, hence the name. The post office was established in 1861, discontinued in 1866, reestablished in 1866 and discontinued again in 1911.[128]

Relief (Mitchell County). A local general store here owned by Squire Peterson sold "Hart's Relief," a popular tonic containing alcohol, giving some users noticeable relief.[129]

Roan Mountain (Mitchell County). The origins of the name of this iconic peak are unclear. Some believe that the mountain turns a roan color when the Catawba rhododendron bloom. Or maybe the mountain takes its name from the mountain ash tree, known in the Old Country as the rowan tree. One theory is that Daniel Boone, hunting throughout the area, left a roan-colored horse to graze here. French explorer André Michaux may have named the mountain after a location in France, the Rhone Valley. Yet another idea comes from the 1869 writings of Charles Lanman, who believed that the snow-covered mountain was a roan color.[130]

Roaring Creek (Avery County). With headwaters between Yellow Mountain and Rye Ridge, the creek flows into the North Toe River in the valley community. Originally called Roan Creek, after Roan Mountain, it was renamed due to the roar produced by the boulders in the creek.[131]

Spear (Avery County). Named for the nearby Spear Tops Mountain, this community's post office was established in 1882 and discontinued in 1953. Spear Tops takes its name from a mountain resembling two spearheads.[132]

Spruce Pine (Mitchell County). The community was originally called Kim Thickets, after Kim McHone, who got lost in a laurel thicket. The post office was established as Rose's Creek in 1856 and changed to Spruce Pine in 1859 for an old tree that stood at the intersection of two roads: the Marion-to-Bakersville Road and the Burnsville-to-Cranberry Road, located near the Old English Inn.[133]

Tipton Hill (Mitchell County). Named in honor of early settler Major Jonathan Tipton III; the post office here was established as Brummett in 1879, changed to Tipton Hill in 1914 and discontinued in 1951.[134]

Toecane (Mitchell County). Cane Creek flows into the North Toe River at this location.[135]

Passenger service has ended in Spruce Pine, but coal trains still occasionally rumble through town. *Dan Barron.*

WINDOM (YANCEY COUNTY). Possibly named in honor of Minnesota congressman, senator and secretary of the treasury William Windom; the post office was established in 1889 and discontinued in 1954.

YELLOW MOUNTAIN (AVERY COUNTY). "There are invariably small spring flowers from the edges of the bald spots. From a distance these green patches seem to be yellow, hence the name." The post office was established in April 1850 and discontinued in December 1866. Another Yellow Mountain post office existed between 1873 and 1879.[136]

Chapter 13

THE HISTORY OF
THE BAKERSVILLE "RIOT"

I t was international news. A fight broke out between a mob and a U.S. deputy marshal at the jail in Bakersville. When the smoke cleared in the nighttime riot, the jailed man, Calvin Snipes, had been hanged by the vigilantes, while seven members of the law enforcement detail were dead and twenty-five of the rioters lay strewn about the town near the jail. The town was "in a state of terror" and in possession of "300 armed men." Later reports placed the number of assailants at five hundred. One newspaper in Nebraska proclaimed the event as the "Greatest Battle in America since the Massacre at Little Big Horn."[137]

The affair all started over moonshine. Aaron Wiseman and Calvin Snipes ran a still and told two brothers, William and Isaac Osborne, the location. William reported the still to the authorities, who destroyed it. Wiseman and Snipes suspected that it was Isaac Osborne who had snitched, and on the night of August 27, 1892, they killed Isaac at his home. Aaron Wiseman was arrested and tried but acquitted due to lack of evidence. Snipes fled the state, was arrested and returned to Mitchell to stand trial. Wishing to avenge the death of his brother and believing that the court would exonerate Snipes, William formed a mob and headed to Bakersville. The group, between three hundred and five hundred, carrying "Winchesters and pistols," contained some of the "best citizens of the county who had become tired and sick at the way things had been done as regards [to] criminals." Seventy-five deputy marshals and local law enforcement officials manned the town. Late in the afternoon of January 4, a demand was made for Snipes by the mob, which was refused. That evening, the mob made for the jail. After ignoring an order to stop, law enforcement opened fire, and "a score" of the mob "went down." The mob closed ranks and with an "old rebel yell" charged the jail, taking aim at the defenders.[138]

A dozen of the defenders were wounded or killed. "There was a short struggle…A few revolver shots, 100 clubbed rifles and all was over. The deputies, with their leader, Sheriff Moomaw, mortally wounded, were in the hands of the mob." Moomaw "was shot twice in the chest and three times through the abdomen." The mob reached the jail cell, knocked in the door, grabbed Snipes, placed a rope around his neck and dragged him through the streets a half mile outside town, where he was hanged. The mob then returned to Bakersville to tend to the dead and wounded. Outside the jail were found twenty-five bodies and, in surrounding buildings, eight more. Thirty were reported wounded. Some newspapers ran a list of both the law enforcement members and mob members killed.[139]

Except, none of that ever happened. Well, almost none of it. Isaac Osborne was killed, and both Aaron Wiseman and Calvin Snipes were arrested and tried for the murder, but they were acquitted on lack of evidence. The riot that captured the attention of the press was all made up by newspaperman J. Wallace Hyams. It appears that Hyams was born in Mitchell County in 1873, the son of Washington Hyams and Harriett Bowman Hyams. J.W. Hyams apparently crossed the mountain into Tennessee and was trying to get a job at the *Daily Comet* in Johnson City. While it is unclear why Hyams wrote the story, the national press devoured it as yet another example of a lawless and corrupt southern Appalachian region. Many of the major newspapers had to print retractions, and some sent reporters to Mitchell County to interview local citizens. Many clamored for Hyams's arrest, forcing him to decamp without settling his hotel bill. He returned to Mitchell County, where he died in 1895.

Chapter 14

THE HISTORY OF THE SPRUCE PINE RIOT

onvict labor was common throughout American history, from colonial times through the early part of the twentieth century. For a certain amount of money and for a certain amount of time, both government entities and private sector corporations could lease men (and later women) convicted of crimes and sentenced to a state penitentiary. Convicts were used to build railroads, improve roads and work on farms. Most were African Americans, and the treatment they received was often brutal. Many locals resented the convicts, as they were perceived to be taking jobs from the local population.

The Toe River Valley never had a large African American population. In the 1860 census, the valley reported just 326 enslaved and free people of color. Only five mountain counties reported fewer. The population of both Blacks and whites grew slowly after the Civil War, but the numbers of both groups dropped significantly after 1910. There simply were not enough jobs in the area to support a large population, and significant numbers of both races moved away. Those outside corporations responsible for building roads and railroads found it cheaper to bring in foreigners or convicts, paying them less than what they would expend to hire local labor. These outside labor forces were placed in both work and prison camps in the area.

This infusion of nonlocal and, at times, foreign outsiders led to a degree of mistrust and even hostility and violence. One such incident came in May 1906 at Camp Six, near the Mitchell-McDowell county line. Italian

Convict workers were brought in to build roads and work on the rails, upsetting locals. *Robert Morgan.*

workers building the railroad threatened to strike if not paid. Negotiations broke down, and gunfire erupted between the sheriff, his deputies and the Italians. At least two Italians were killed in what became known as the "Tally War." Another episode occurred in February 1922 when a white convict on a chain gang in Mitchell County at Boonford stole two sticks of dynamite and threw them at the guards, hoping to create a distraction so he could escape. One stick did not go off, while the other exploded nowhere near the guards. Another attempt from the prison camp in Mitchell County was successful in July 1923. Four Black convicts overpowered a guard, took his weapons and escaped into Tennessee. A "battle royal" ensued when they were tracked down; one prisoner was killed and another wounded. The prison camp at Boonford recorded more prison breaks or escapes than all other camps in North Carolina combined. In one instance, in May 1922, twenty-one of the fifty-two prisoners escaped from the camp, possibly with the help of some of their guards. Another six escaped a month later, including Sol and Latt Slagle, convicted of murdering a man in Buncombe County. These escapees were dependent on food and clothes stolen from local families.[140]

An event in the fall of 1923 pushed the patience of local people to the limit. An inmate, John Goss, who previously had been found guilty of assaulting a woman in Wilmington, left the convict camp near Spruce Pine to go to work on the road crew on the morning of September 26. He slipped off during the day and assaulted Mrs. Alice Thomas. As word of the attack spread throughout the area, men under Deputy Sheriff Mack Buchanan armed themselves and began to comb the woods, looking for the assailant. The town of Spruce Pine offered a $500 reward for the attacker's capture. Goss fled south and was arrested in Hickory three days later.[141]

Undoubtedly having the recent escapes on their minds, a local armed mob formed and moved toward the convict camp outside Spruce Pine. One account stated that the citizens asked the convicts to leave. "All left without disorder," and everything was quiet in Spruce Pine. Another account stated that "Town Marshal L.H. Wright and other citizens" met the group on the Spruce Pine bridge and "by persuasion, caused them to desist." Yet another group, a larger group, went to the camp the following morning and ordered the convicts to leave town. "The leaders of the mob made no loud threats. They merely assured the negroes that their presence was not desired and that the next train should find them in transit," reported the *Asheville Citizen Times*. On September 29, the newspaper reported, "Not one negro remained in Spruce Pine." Between 150 and 175 convict laborers had been loaded on a train and shipped out of the area. One newspaper reported that they were headed for Tennessee, while another stated that some of the workers had arrived in Spartanburg, South Carolina.[142]

Word arrived in Raleigh of a "riot," and North Carolina governor Cameron Morrison called out the National Guard, sending two companies, along with Adjutant General J. Van. B. Metts, to Spruce Pine. Newspapers were quick to pick up on the idea of a "riot." The Black "laborers" were "driven out of Spruce Pine by an armed crowd, which took this method of expressing its wrath over the assault," reported the *Charlotte Observer*. Local citizens were "enraged," reported a newspaper in Nebraska. Yet the episode of a violent mob attacking the convicts—murdering, burning and looting in mob fashion—never appears to have happened. The Black laborers and convicts were indeed forcibly removed. According to one account, Black men were given time to pack their belongings and then escorted to the depot, where they were ordered onto a train. Metts and the National Guard troops found "no evidence of mob spirit here." Yet at the same time, one newspaper reported that an armed crowd was marching up and down the street. Metts ordered any man found carrying weapons or "handling liquor" arrested.[143]

Left: North Carolina governor Cameron Morrison ordered the National Guard to deal with the riot. *State Archives of North Carolina.*

Below: Downtown Spruce Pine appears here in 1925, just two years after the riots. *State Archives of North Carolina.*

With Goss back in the state prison in Raleigh and identified by Thomas as her attacker, Governor Morrison set in motion a speedy trial. He ordered a special session of the Superior Court to be held in Bakersville on October 22, 1923. More National Guard companies arrived, and the Mitchell County justice of the peace issued warrants for the arrest of fourteen local men, charged with unlawful assembly, committing a riot and conspiracy to unlawfully assemble, riot and commit assaults. Twelve men were arrested, and all but two bonded out. A handful of those displaced returned on October 1, with the National Guard providing security. There were no attempts by local people to prohibit their return, and slowly the crews working on the roads and in the mines returned. Governor Morrison ordered the National Guard companies to return to their homes on October 7.[144]

Except for charging additional men with conspiracy, unlawful assembly and riot, the matter quickly disappeared from the state press until Goss's trial. Judge T.B. Finley presided over the trial at the courthouse in Bakersville. One company of National Guard troops returned for the proceedings. An estimated six hundred people gathered for the trial, but some were sent out of the courtroom when Judge Hayes dismissed women and those under sixteen. After the jury was selected, the trial began at 3:00 p.m., lasting about an hour. The jury deliberated about five minutes before returning a guilty verdict. Conviction of a capital crime, like rape, mandated a death sentence then, and Goss was sentenced to be electrocuted on November 30, 1923. Goss was escorted by the National Guard to Hickory and then by state prison officials to Raleigh. He did not seek an appeal. His death was postponed until December 7, and it was reported that he confessed his crime to a minister.[145]

The story of the Spruce Pine riot is often misconstrued in print. A 1999 book on the writings of NAACP lawyer James W. Johnson noted that "an armed rob of two hundred whites was rounding up colored citizens of Spruce Pine." No record of a Spruce Pine citizen being "rounded up" exists, only of convicts at various work camps. Doug McGuinn wrote that this event was "the worst race riot in Mitchell County." There was not much of a riot. Elliot Jaspin wrote that the original group that went looking for Goss after the attack was "searching for vengeance" but left out the fact that the deputy sheriff was with the group. The mob was "heavily armed and spoiling for a fight…most likely a group of angry, gun toting backwoodsmen" ready to murder any Black men who did not leave. Except no one was murdered, and while the Black convicts were ushered out of town, there were no reports of other acts of violence. The events in September and October in Mitchell County were tragic for those involved but not an actual riot. Locals were wrong in forcing out the convict workers. At the same time, locals could have had those jobs if the outside companies had been willing to pay a decent wage for the work instead of relying on cheap convict labor.[146]

Chapter 15

HOTELS ABOVE THE CLOUDS

There once were numerous hotels in the Toe River Valley area. While tourists have always found their way into the area, the advent of the railroad opened the valley for those seeking to enjoy the unbeatable summer climate as well as fishing and hunting. Many tourists stayed with families, but others preferred hotels, particularly in the last quarter of the nineteenth century. Some families expanded their homes into inns or boardinghouses for visitors, such as the Dolph Wilson Hotel in Eskota (Yancey County) and the Weld House (Avery County). Unfortunately, only one of these mountain grande dames still exists in the Toe River Valley.

CLOUDLAND HOTEL

Probably the most famous of the long-gone hotels in the Toe River Valley area was Cloudland Hotel. Constructed on Roan Mountain, half of the hotel was in Mitchell County and half was in Tennessee. John T. Wilder, who owned forty-six thousand acres in the Roan Mountain area, was the impetus behind the hotel. In 1877, he directed the first twenty-room, spruce-log structure to be built. The second, much larger, frame structure was built nearby and opened in 1886. This structure, officially known as Cloudland Hotel, had 166 rooms. Visitors arrived via the ET&WNC at the Roan Mountain station, where a hack took them up the mountain. Cloudland

Cloudland Hotel, atop Roan Mountain, attracted guests from all over the eastern United States. *Library of Congress.*

Hotel was steam-heated, necessary at 6,394 feet above sea level. Rooms rented for $2.50 per day. There was a dance hall and golf course, and the large dining table had a white line painted down the middle, with Tennessee on one side and North Carolina on the other. On staff were a doctor, baker, butcher and barber. For a variety of reasons, such as the short time it was opened each year and the expense of upkeep, Cloudland closed shortly after the turn of the century and was abandoned in 1910. Eventually, an auction was held, and people purchased individual rooms, including the furniture and the woodwork. Pieces of the old Cloudland Hotel can still be found in homes today. Parts of the foundation and a historical marker commemorate the hotel at Roan Mountain State Park.[147]

Topliff Hotel

Opening in 1901, Spruce Pine's Topliff Hotel was constructed by Z. Taylor Phillips, who named it the Umatilla House. In 1917, Phillips placed it up for sale, stating that it had thirty rooms, a small cottage and a private water works and was the only hotel in town. The property was purchased in 1920 by C.H. Topliff, who enlarged it with a three-story wing and changed the name. In addition, the Topliff Hotel had a grand ballroom and several offices and hosted many civic groups, like the Rotary; it was also the local bus terminal. On August 6, 1948, the hotel was destroyed by fire.[148]

Altapass Inn

In the early twentieth century, it often took a railroad to bring a town to life or to create an entire town. Altapass, created by the Clinchfield Railroad, was, according to one historian, the line's "premier tourist stop…with a golf course, two resort hotels, and a railroad boarding house." Advertisements began to appear in the spring of 1910 in southern newspapers promoting the Altapass Inn, one of those resort hotels. One stated that patrons could "stand on [a] mountain top, over 3,000 feet above the sea level, and commune with the weeping souls above." Another in 1913 used the phrase "Altapass Inn Above the Land of the Sky." In 1916, it was the "Queen of the Summitland." The inn boasted modern plumbing, a bowling alley, billiards, trap shooting, a house physician and a ballroom with orchestra. Guests from the surrounding towns and cities could board a train to the Altapass Inn and, after a night of dancing, return the next day. The inn was sold to a Florida investment group in 1925. Demand to stay at one of the premier resorts in the Blue Ridge was so great in 1926 that the inn opened one month early. Unfortunately, it caught fire on May 19, 1926, was a total loss and was never rebuilt.[149]

Banner Elk Hotel

The Banner Elk Hotel did not start life as a hotel but rather was built around 1856 as a home for Edwin Banner; it was later purchased by Lorenzo Dow Lowe. As the Lowe family expanded, so did the house. With the growth of Banner Elk, the owners saw a need to provide lodging for people coming to enjoy the cool summers, the trout fishing and hunting

Top: Spruce Pine's Topliff Hotel was the center of the town's social life from the early 1900s until burning in 1948. *Daniel Barron.*

Middle: Altapass Inn, constructed in 1916, was destroyed by fire in 1926. *University of North Carolina–Chapel Hill, Wilson Library Special Collections.*

Bottom: Altapass Inn visitors bowled, played billiards and ate ice cream. *University of North Carolina–Chapel Hill, Wilson Library Special Collections.*

in the winter months. For fifty years, the Banner Elk Hotel entertained guests and, like many other hotels of the time, served as a community focal point. Mary Elder recalled hearing a radio for the first time at the hotel. The Women's Club of Banner Elk was organized there in 1930. The Men's Service Club followed in 1931. In May 1939, the junior and senior banquet for the Grace Hospital School of Nursing was held at the Banner Elk Hotel. The hotel stopped serving boarders in 1973. It was added to the National Register of Historic Places in 2000, but that did not save it: the hotel was razed by several fire departments in training exercises. Townhomes were built on the site.[150]

Pinnacle Inn

Banner Elk was a happening place in the 1920s. People flocked to the hamlet in the summer, staying at the Banner Elk Hotel or the Old Turnpike Inn. As the country struggled through the Great Depression years in 1932, Lees-McRae Institute chose to open the Tennessee Dorm in the summers as the Pinnacle Inn, providing an opportunity for female students to earn money for the upcoming school year and gain business experience. When the school became coed, male students worked as porters; maintained the golf course, swimming pool, tennis and croquet courts; and worked on the farm. At the time, the Pinnacle was declared the highest resort, in elevation, east of the Rocky Mountains, with tennis, croquet, hiking, boating and fishing and access to the college's library—but no dancing, at least at first. In 1931, the Pinnacle Inn hosted the Sportsman's Mountain Trout Dinner. The main feature of the seven-course meal was trout from Howard Marmon's fishery. Professor I.G. Greer entertained the guests with mountain folk songs and ballads. The Pinnacle Inn closed in the 1960s. The Tennessee Residence Hall still provides housing for students at Lees-McRae College.[151]

Eseeola Inn/Lodge

The community of Linville was created in 1891. While there were several inns, the centerpiece was the Eseeola Inn, constructed with a chestnut bark exterior. The bark trend continued to other houses and buildings in the community, including the LRR Depot. Before the LRR was constructed,

The original 1892 Eseeola Lodge, in the Linville community, burned in 1936. *Avery County Historical Museum.*

a coach met visitors in Cranberry at the terminus of the ET&WNC, or they came from Blowing Rock on the Yonahlossee Road. The Eseeola was one of the finest establishments in Western North Carolina but struggled initially. It took a few years before the right clientele was attracted. Eseeola offered golf, archery, fishing, lawn bowling and horseback riding. Additions were soon needed, and the property grew to accommodate 110 guests. There was a physician and telephone operator when the hotel was open. On Sunday, June 28, 1936, the Eseeola caught fire and was a total loss. Reservations for the upcoming season were moved to the Chestnut Lodge, located directly across from the Eseeola Inn. This structure was built in 1929, and after the 1936 fire, it was renamed the Eseeola Lodge. Besides the inn/lodge, Eseeola also had North Carolina's first golf course. Golf was being played in Eseeola as early as the summer in 1895. The course had nine holes that were played twice to achieve a round of eighteen. Guests teed off in front of the inn at "The Fountain," with the last hole being named "Arthur's Seat." Donald Ross designed a new course in 1922. Eseeola is still in operation in 2023.[152]

The 1830s Nu-Wray was once Burnsville's cultural center. *Author's collection.*

Constructed in the late 1700s, the Old English Inn is considered one of the state's oldest and largest log buildings. *Author's collection.*

Nu-Wray Inn

Constructed in the new county of Yancey in 1833, the Nu-Wray Inn is one of the oldest in the western part of the state. Originally, it had eight rooms and was a trading post operated by Bacchus Smith. Then it was purchased by Milton Penland and, in 1870, by Garrett D. Ray and known as the Ray Hotel for decades. Located in the heart of Burnsville, the hotel witnessed much of the town's history. Political rallies took place in front of the hotel, leading to an 1894 fight between the supporters of the two parties. Among the rumored famous figures who have stayed at the Nu-Wray are Mark Twain, Thomas Wolfe, Christopher Reeve, Elvis Presley and Jimmy Carter. By 1956, it had forty rooms. As of 2023, the Nu-Wray Inn is undergoing renovations.[153]

Old English Inn

It is unclear when the Old English Inn was built. Some want to place its construction prior to the American Revolution—unlikely, with raids by the Cherokees in 1776. The Old English Inn was constructed by the Rowe family most likely in the years right after the American Revolution, connected to the influx of new settlers swarming into the area. There was a ford of the North Toe River nearby, and several trails, probably Native American, crossed near the cabin. These became the roads from Marion to Bakersville and from Cranberry to Burnsville. According to one article, the property was owned by James Bailey, who in 1866 sold it to Isaac English. The cabin expanded over time. There was also a mica-grading cabin added to the original structure. The Old English Inn survives today as a private residence and is believed to be the state's oldest and largest log structure.[154]

Chapter 16

CHILDSVILLE

The Lost County Seat of Mitchell County

Yancey County has only had one county seat: Burnsville. Avery County has had two: Elk Park and then, after the courthouse was finished in 1913, Newland. The leadership of Mitchell County had met in a variety of places just in the first decade of the county's existence.

After several years of wrangling, Mitchell County was formed in February 1861. When the General Assembly created Mitchell County, it also decreed that the county court of Pleas and Quarter Sessions was to be "held in the house of Eben Childs on the tenth Monday after the fourth Monday in March." At this meeting, they were to elect a clerk, sheriff, coroner, register of deeds and entry taker, surveyor, county solicitor and constables. Seven men from the surrounding counties were appointed to a group to select a suitable place for the seat of justice. On October 17, 1861, Lysander D. Childs and Eben Childs donated fifty acres "for the location thereon of a permanent seat of justice…two acres for a public graveyard one acre for the site of a public school building, and one-half acres…to each of the following denominations for the erection thereon of church buildings; to wit: Episcopalians, Presbyterians, Methodist and Baptist."[155]

In 1850, the Childs family of Massachusetts purchased some of the old Bright property, settling along the North Toe River. The Childsville Post Office was established on April 4, 1850. One visitor in 1857 described Childsville as being in a "beautiful valley on Tow [*sic*] River, which abounds with the speckled trout so admired by Mr. Clingman…a little earthly paradise; and besides its beauties, capitalists may there find rare chances for investments,

Dr. Ebenezer Childs, founder of the now-lost community of Childsville, came to present-day Avery County in the 1850s. *Claudia Childs McGough.*

and sportsmen, abundance of game, from the smallest *bug* to the biggest *bear.*"[156]

Probably in honor of South Carolina senator John C. Calhoun, the General Assembly changed the name of Childsville to Calhoun. An auction was scheduled on February 17, 1862, for town lots. The courthouse was a barn that belonged to the Childs family. However, not all was well in Calhoun. The Superior Court met in Calhoun in the fall of 1861, fall of 1862 and fall of 1863. The Court of Pleas and Sessions, which met quarterly, met in Calhoun in June 1861 and the fall of 1863; in the "Baptist Meeting House on Bear Creek" for its fall 1861 term and March, June and December 1863 terms; in an undisclosed location for the December 1861 term, March, June and December 1862 terms and March 1864 term; and in Bakersville in September 1862. According to one historian, no one liked the location of Calhoun, and "at the first session of the legislature after the Civil War," the county seat was moved to a community called Davis, now known as Bakersville.[157]

After the county seat was moved, Calhoun reverted to being called Childsville. The post office was discontinued in June 1877. Many members of the Childs family relocated to Lincoln County and Columbia, South Carolina, following the Civil War. The property along the North Toe River was sold to the Wiseman family. At some point, not long after the county seat was moved, the "huge log building was torn down." There is nothing left of Childsville today. No buildings, not even a historical marker, denote the former county seat. It is truly a piece of hidden history.[158]

Chapter 17

STRUCTURES WITH A HIDDEN HISTORY

WPA and CCC Buildings

There is an old story that says poor mountain people never knew that there was a Great Depression. While this might have been true for a few families, most people in the Toe River Valley were keenly aware of the hard times gripping the nation. There were several causes of the Great Depression, including the stock market crash of 1929, overproduction of consumer goods and regional banking collapses. These events collided with poor federal decisions, such as the Smoot-Hawley Tariff and raised tariffs on imported goods while interest rates remained high. Nationwide, unemployment was over 25 percent. Industrial production declined 47 percent, and the GDP fell 30 percent in one year. Statewide, 98 banks closed in the 1920s, and another 194 closed between 1930 and 1933.[159]

Equally hard hit was the Toe River Valley. The Cranberry Iron Works in Avery County closed in 1929. The summer of 1930 brought drought, and conditions remained dry through 1934. Massive fires sprang up across the area. Banks began closing; Citizens Bank of Burnsville closed in December 1930 due to "heavy withdrawals." The Citizens Bank in Elk Park likewise closed. By August, local farmers had trouble finding markets for their produce, and the products they were selling were for reduced prices. One year later, one newspaper reported that Yancey County school officials were forced to reduce school expenditures by 25 percent over three years. Bessie Willis, teaching school in the Dark Ridge area of Avery County in the fall of 1931, recalled in her memoir that a month after term started, she had not received a check. She wrote to the school superintendent,

The Works Progress Administration employed hundreds of men and some women in scores of Toe River Valley projects. *W.R. Trivett Collection.*

thinking that it might have been lost in the mail. "I am sorry to tell you that the county has no funds at present to pay its teachers. We will do the best we can by you," Teague wrote back. The next month, she finally received her pay for July.[160]

President Herbert Hoover implemented some limited federal assistance programs to help alleviate the suffering In January 1933, $4,000 had been allocated to Mitchell County for relief work. The funds were to be used to employ local people to beautify cemeteries, clean school grounds, improve roads and provide general cleaning of towns. Three hundred men were employed in this program about the first week of January.[161]

Franklin D. Roosevelt was elected as president in 1932. He carried over some of Hoover's strategies but also implemented a new package of government plans. The New Deal was a series of programs, public work projects, financial reforms and regulations authorized by Roosevelt between 1933 and 1939. Some programs, like the Works Progress Administration (WPA) and the Civilian Conservation Corps (CCC), helped local people. Others, like the portions of the National Industrial Recovery Administration that set minimum wages and maximum hours, along with price controls, were ruled unconstitutional by the Supreme Court. While there were dozens of programs, two dominate local historical memory: the CCC and the WPA.

More than twenty-seven thousand North Carolinians served in the CCC in sixty-one camps across the state. The CCC recruited young single men between seventeen and twenty-five years of age. They were paid thirty dollars per month, twenty-five of which was sent to their families. The young men wore uniforms, lived in camps and worked in companies of one hundred to two hundred. Among their assigned tasks were digging firebreaks and building fire towers, restoring historic areas and planting seedlings to hold the soil and prevent erosion of areas stripped of timber. One of the local CCC camps was located in the Black Mountains at Mount Mitchell State Park. Those stationed there planted Fraser fir and Norway spruce trees, built the concession stand and visitor's center and then added flush toilets and a new water and sewer system. The companies stationed at Mount Mitchell also constructed the Carolina Hemlocks Campground and Recreation area, including the looping road, picnic tables, amphitheater with bonfire pit and three miles of hiking trails. Another camp was established near Bakersville. Named the Floyd Ramsey Camp, this company operated under the supervision of the Tennessee

Some WPA projects included the Mount Mitchell visitor's center, restrooms, museum and gift shop. *State Archives of North Carolina.*

Yancey County's Clearmont community school was a WPA project. *Author's collection.*

Valley Authority and was tasked with conservation programs, like flood control, soil erosion control and reforestation. The Mitchell County camp opened in July 1935 and was disbanded in October 1937. Yet another project concerned fire watch towers. The 1930s saw the construction of towers on Hawshaw Mountain and Big Chestnut Knob in Avery County and Devil's Nest and Roan High Knob in Mitchell County. In 1942, Congress ceased funding the CCC, redirecting the funds toward the war effort. Nationwide, more than 3 million young men took part in the CCC, planting more than 3 billion trees and working in more than eight hundred parks. Not only did the program put money into the pockets of local families, but it also trained many young men in various job skills and accomplished needed tasks. For some, the CCC provided adventures in new places and gave them a taste of what life would be like when the United States entered World War II.[162]

Some of the more visible surviving pieces of the New Deal are the numerous WPA schools spread out across the Toe River Valley. Between 1935 and 1940, the WPA employed 125,000 men and women across the state, completing 3,984 projects. Not only did the WPA build schools, but it also constructed sewing rooms, conducted cemetery surveys, completed theater projects, created murals and recorded slave narratives, along with building swimming pools, gyms, hospitals, sewers, community halls, stadiums and armories. Locally, WPA funds were allocated to improve Hardscrabble Road in Yancey County and Fork Mountain Road in Mitchell County; construct a lunchroom at an Avery County school; and pay librarians in Mitchell County. There were five WPA schools in Yancey County: Bald Creek, Bee Log, Clearmont, Burnsville and Micaville. Six were built in Avery County: Riverside, Newland, Banner Elk, Beech Mountain, Crossnore and Elk Park. There were two in Mitchell County: Micaville and Tipton Hill (the schools at Buladean, Ledger, Spruce Pine and Glen Ayre had classrooms added to preexisting structures). Some of the schools survive today as community centers. A few, like Crossnore, have been torn down.[163]

Chapter 18

HOLIDAY HISTORY

White House Christmas Trees from the Toe River Valley

W ith the country in the throes of the Great Depression, 1934 is not a year that typically stands out in a positive sense. Yet it was in 1934 that the first Christmas tree from the Toe River Valley headed to the White House. According to a Raleigh newspaper, two large balsam trees from Avery County were sent to the White House at the request of President Franklin D. Roosevelt. Ed Robbins, owner of the Gardens of the Blue Ridge in Pineola, worked with a man appointed by the White House to select the trees. "Each tree is 21 feet high. They will be placed on both sides of the walk leading to the White House and will be used for the Christmas celebrations." Lute Clark and Corbitt Johnson were responsible for moving the trees.[164]

That honor does not seem to have been bestowed on a tree from the Toe River Valley again until 1971. In a nationwide competition, Kermit Johnson of Crossnore won the contest sponsored by the U.S. Christmas Tree Growers Association. An eight-foot Fraser fir grown on his farm was selected to be placed in the Blue Room in the White House in December of that year.[165]

Christmas trees as a viable agricultural crop first came to the United States in 1901 when W.V. McGalliard planted twenty-five thousand Norway spruce trees in New Jersey. By the late 1940s, at least 100,000 acres were being used to grow Christmas trees, including 40,000 acres in Pennsylvania. In the South, the eastern red cedar, often found in the woods and along fence rows, was a popular Christmas tree. The commercial aspect began in cities, where residents did not have access to the farmer's fence row. Fraser firs became the

Julie Nixon Eisenhower and Pat Nixon pose in the White House Blue Room with the 1971 Christmas tree from the Toe River Valley. *Nixon White House Photographs.*

Ira Simpson and G.G. Paris harvest Christmas trees on Roan Mountain, 1952. *State Archives of North Carolina.*

most popular Christmas tree in the mid-twentieth century. Many were cut locally on Roan Mountain and up Roaring Creek. T.P. Dellinger, agriculture teacher at Crossnore High School, began talking about growing Christmas trees locally in the mid-1940s. Several local farmers embraced the new crop, including Claude Pittman, Ira Vance, Lindsey Daniels, Herman Dellinger and Jack W. Wiseman.[166]

In 1970, more than 150,000 Christmas trees were sold from Avery County, and nearly 500,000 seedlings were planted. Two years later, Avery County was proclaimed as the "Christmas Tree Capital." The Christmas tree industry was an $86 million industry in 2017, with North Carolina producing 5.4 million trees in 2021. North Carolina has provided 14 White House Blue Room Christmas trees since 1961. Avery County trees were selected in 1971 as well as 1990 (R. Bruce Lacey and Michael Lacey), 1993 (Wayne Ayers) and 2018 (Larry Smith). Trees from the Toe River Valley have also been used numerous times in the governor's residence and state capitol in Raleigh. Christmas trees from the area have allowed people across the eastern United States to have a piece of the Toe River Valley every holiday season.[167]

Chapter 19

LOST ATTRACTIONS OF THE
TOE RIVER VALLEY

The Toe River Valley has numerous natural attractions: high mountains, waterfalls, plants and flowers. With the advancement of railroads and better roads for automobiles, entrepreneurs began looking for ways to cater to visitors. Some of these were simple, like roadside stands to sell honey. Other were bizarre, like a bear in a cage at the Crossnore service station. Many other businesses are not listed, such as bowling alleys, community pools and music venues once popular in communities across the region and now long gone.

SEVEN DEVILS SKI RESORT/SKI HAWKSNEST

It is uncertain when someone first donned a pair of wooden slats and headed down a snowy hill in Western North Carolina. However, a January 1937 newspaper reported, "Not all the skiing is done in Switzerland, New England and Sun Valley, Idaho." The article told of a "ski colony" in North Carolina, inhabited by students from Lees-McRae College in Banner Elk, and photos featured several with their skis. Their favorite slope was Hemlock Hill, overlooking the mill pond on campus. Snow in January 1940 led those early pioneers to Beech Mountain as well.[168]

References to skiing disappeared during the World War II years. However, they began to filter back into the press not long after the war ended in 1945. Some were downhill skiing on Roan Mountain and, in 1951, were discussing

Snow skiing in Banner Elk became popular in the 1930s. *Lees-McRae College.*

installing a tow rope. The first North Carolina commercial operation opened in Haywood County in 1961, followed by Blowing Rock Ski Lodge in Watauga County the next year. In 1967, the slopes at Seven Devils, just inside Avery County, began business. With the addition of the slopes at Beech Mountain and Sugar Mountain, opening in 1968 and 1969, Banner Elk became known as the "Ski Capital of the South."[169]

In 1982, the Seven Devils Ski Resort area was purchased by Jon Reynolds and rebranded as Ski Hawksnest. It remained open until 2008, when the owners, citing conflicts with the Town of Seven Devils, closed. The site later reopened as one of the best snow tubing sites in the eastern United States.[170]

THE LAND OF OZ

A theme park dedicated to the world of *The Wizard of Oz* on a mountain in Avery County? Why not?! The Robbins brothers, building a ski resort on Beech Mountain in the mid-1960s, were looking to add something to attract guests in the summer. They turned to designer Jack Pentes, who, upon touring the site, was struck by the gnarled and twisted trees shaped by the harsh winter winds, reminiscent of those in the 1939 movie *The Wizard of Oz*, based on the book by L. Frank Baum.

The Land of Oz theme park celebrated *The Wizard of Oz* atop Beech Mountain. *Author's collection.*

Construction on a unique park soon began, and in June 1970, the Land of Oz opened on the top of Beech Mountain. Visitors began their adventures in the Oz Museum, seeing original movie props that had been purchased at an auction. Then it was to the Gale farm, where a storm whisked guests to Oz. Dorothy escorted visitors along the Yellow Brick Road, meeting the Tin Man, Cowardly Lion, Scarecrow and the Wicked Witch of the West along the way. In the Emerald City, guests could dine, shop and enjoy the fifteen-minute grand finale. Then Dorothy and Toto boarded a hot air balloon and sailed away. That first year, 139,000 people visited. A recession and the mid-1970s gas crunch hurt attendance. In December 1975, vandals broke in, stole artifacts and set fire to the theater, destroying many costumes. With just 60,000 visitors in 1980, the park closed. The site sat vacant, overgrown, with additional vandalism and fires for more than a decade. By the mid-1990s, the park was reopening one day a year—the Autumn at Oz event. Although the event has continued, the heyday of the actual park is part of history, with bits and pieces of the yellow brick road and other features peeking out as reminders of the past.[171]

CAROLINA THEATRE

During the golden age of the silver screen, there were quite a few theaters in the Toe River Valley. Avery County had at least five: two in Crossnore and one each in Newland, Banner Elk and Elk Park. Plus, movies were shown on a wall at the Tar Heel Mica facility in Plumtree. Burnsville had at least two theaters and a few drive-ins. Bakersville had the Mars Theater. While Spruce Pine had the Piedmont Theater and Baker Theater, probably the theater best remembered was the Carolina Theatre on Lower Street in Spruce Pine. Construction began on the Carolina Theater in the fall of 1937. *Something to Sing About*, a musical/comedy starring James Cagney and Evelyn Daw, was the first movie shown when the theater opened in December that year. O.D. Calhoun, who operated several regional theaters, and J. Myron Houston, a merchant and musician, teamed up to create the *Carolina Barn Dance*. It started out as a talent program and later evolved into a nationally syndicated old-time music show on the Liberty Broadcasting System. The concert was performed and recorded on Friday nights and then rebroadcast on Saturdays. Lulu Belle and Scotty were favorites at the *Carolina Barn Dance*. Other performers of notoriety were Kitty Wells, Tennessee Ernie Ford, Bill Monroe, Patsy Cline and Chet Atkins. When the Liberty Broadcasting

Left: The Carolina Theater in Spruce Pine featured movies and the nationally syndicated *Carolina Barn Dance*. *Author's collection.*

Opposite: Daniel Boone VI built a scaled-down version of a steam locomotive, a village and museum. *State Archives of North Carolina.*

System folded in 1954, the *Carolina Barn Dance* ceased airing. The Carolina Theater continued showing movies for the next few decades, shuttering as a movie theater in the mid-1990s. It has sat empty since the early 2000s, but there are plans to refurbish and reopen it.[172]

Booneville Railroad, Forge and Museum

"The Booneville Train will be in operation every Saturday…and on Sunday…located opposite the Mt. Mitchell Motel," ran an advertisement in a Yancey County newspaper in 1962. Daniel Boone VI built a 1.5-inch scale steam locomotive, an exact copy of a Union Pacific 484 Baldwin engine, beginning in 1957. Boone then built four Pullman cars capable of pulling thirty-six passengers, seven hundred feet of track and a village and museum. The museum contained both ironwork made by Boone and original pieces that dated back two centuries. The train was open seasonally for several years. After Boone's death, the train passed to a relative, was

sold at an estate sale in 1989 and was eventually sold at a Barrett-Jackson Auction in 2019.[173]

LOST GOLF COURSES OF THE TOE RIVER VALLEY

With more than sixteen thousand courses in the United States, golf is widely popular. As of 2023, there are eleven public and private courses in the Toe River Valley, the majority in Avery County. However, there are also at least five area courses that no longer exist. The first course was laid out in 1895 in Linville, a few years before the course at Pinehurst. Players teed off near the Hemlock Hedges cottage and played through the empty lots surrounding the community. As new homes were built, the course was adjusted. Fairways were not trimmed and contained rocks and boulders. The tees were mounds, and only the greens were mowed. There were just nine holes until 1900, when four additional holes were added to the north of Lenoir Park. Caddies were often local young men. Plans for a new eighteen-hole course, designed by Donald Ross, were developed in 1924, and the course was dedicated on August 18, 1928. The old course was gradually forgotten. Cloudland Hotel,

Golf was played in Linville as early as 1895 on the Tanglewood Golf Course. *Avery County Historical Museum.*

The Mount Mitchell Camp for Boys was one of many mid-twentieth-century local camps. *State Archives of North Carolina.*

sitting high up Roan Mountain, had a course. Due to the altitude, special balls had to be used. More information about the course at Cloudland Hotel seems lost to history. Lees-McRae College in Banner Elk also had a course. Students constructed a nine-hole course that opened in the summer of 1930. This course was located on the grounds of the Grandfather Home for Children. Once again, this course seems lost to history. Golf was first mentioned at Altapass in 1914. There was a tournament that year, with the men's winner receiving an engraved cup made of copper, with pewter handles, and the ladies' winner receiving a silver cup. The sport of golf seems to disappear from Altapass after 1926 when the inn burned. At least one other Yancey County golf course existed but is now lost. Camp Mount Mitchell for Boys advertised golf as one of its draws starting in 1933. With a nine-hole course, the boys competed for championships like adults. Campers from Camp Mount Mitchell for Girls also used the course, which was located off modern US-19E, behind the Ingles grocery store. Nothing remains of the camp or the golf course.[174]

Robertson Museum

Dr. W.B. Robertson was typical of the early twentieth-century doctors in the Toe River Valley, spending a great deal of time out in the community making house calls. Robertson also had an eye for history, collecting items during his travels. He even built a small museum next to his office in Burnsville. A visitor in 1938 described the museum as having displays on minerals found in North Carolina; a quilt with the names of more than three hundred men from Yancey County who fought in World War I; locally made firearms, spinning wheels and farm implements; foreign coins; Native American artifacts; pioneer clothing; and the skull of the first man electrocuted in North Carolina. Robertson's museum was the first museum in the Toe River Valley. In 1948, it was announced that Robertson was donating his collection to Yancey County, but the collection's fate remains a mystery.[175]

Chapter 20

HOLLYWOOD HISTORY IN THE
TOE RIVER VALLEY

An estimated five thousand or more films, TV shows and commercials have been filmed in North Carolina. A few filmmakers have brought the Toe River Valley to millions of viewers.

Then I'll Come Back to You (1916). Starring Alice Brady and Jack Sherrill, much of this movie was filmed in the Asheville area. The drama was based on a novel of the same name by Larry Evans. The big fight scene was filmed in Pensacola in Yancey County, at the Carolina Spruce Company. The commissary and mill, along with Black Mountain Railroad, were all backdrops. Several local men were extras. The world premiere of the movie was held in Pensacola. Unfortunately, a copy of this early film does not seem to survive.[176]

Where the Lilies Bloom (1974). Bill and Vera Cleaver wrote *Where the Lilies Bloom*, released in 1970, which received the Newberry Book Award. The novel tells the story of the Luther family, orphan siblings trying to survive in Appalachia. The movie starred Harry Dean Stanton, Rance Howard, Julie Gholson and Jan Smithers. Music was performed by Earl Scruggs. There was an extensive use of locals in Avery and Watauga Counties and of local scenes, such as the Elk Park Elementary School. *Where the Lilies Bloom* was met with good reviews.[177]

Winter People (1989). Set amid the Great Depression, *Winter People* used many Avery County locations and local extras. The movie, based on John Ehle's book *The Winter People*, starred Kurt Russell, Kelly McGillis and Lloyd Bridges and was mostly shot on location in Plumtree, along

The 1989 film adaptation of John Ehle's *Winter People* was partly filmed along the North Toe River. *Avery County Historical Museum.*

the North Toe River. Miss Kay's cabin is still in Plumtree (although on private property). The old Burleson Store in Plumtree was revamped for the movie, and the gym at the old Cranberry School was used to store and build props. The clock tower constructed for the movie is no longer standing. Tombstones for one scene were crafted by local stonecutter Doug Buchanan. Five different local babies were used to play the protagonist's child. The movie premiered at the Carolina Theatre in Spruce Pine in April 1989, with some actors attending.[178]

The Last of the Mohicans (1992). Based on James Fenimore Cooper's 1826 novel, part of the Leatherstocking Tales, this film takes place in 1757 during the French and Indian War and is set in eastern New York State. There were many locations across Western North Carolina that served as locations for the stunning film adaptation. Part of the river rescue scene was filmed on the Nolichucky River, above Huntdale, although it is unclear if this footage was used for the film. Another scene was shot above Linville Falls, both on the trail leading from the visitor's center and along the Linville River.[179]

Forrest Gump (1994). Winston Groom's *Forrest Gump*, released in 1986, originally only sold thirty thousand copies. After being adapted to film, the book sold 1 million more. The film adaptation—starring Tom Hanks, Robin Wright, Gary Sinise and Sally Field—follows Gump as he teaches Elvis Presley how to dance, plays football at the University of Alabama, fights in the Vietnam War, meets presidents, becomes a table tennis champion and unknowingly exposes the Watergate scandal. Forrest later runs across America, including a visit to Grandfather Mountain. Forrest Gump Curve, where the scene was filmed, is marked. *Forrest Gump* was the highest-grossing movie in 1994 and earned numerous awards, including the Golden Globe for Best Motion Picture Drama and the Academy Award for Best Picture.[180]

Chapter 21

THE PENLAND SCHOOL

Inspired by necessity" is the phrase used to describe the craft industry in southern Appalachia. There was a serious decline in locally made products with the arrival of the railroad and the advent of large mail-order companies in the late nineteenth and early twentieth centuries. The craft industry revival is often credited to the arrival of outside college-educated teachers and Christian missionaries, who realized that locally made products could be sold in distant markets, raising revenue for educational ventures. Lucy Morgan was one such leader.[181]

Born in 1889 in Macon County, North Carolina, Lucy Morgan received her teaching certification at the Central Michigan Normal School, and for several years, she taught in Michigan, Illinois and Montana, while studying at the University of Chicago. In 1920, she arrived at the Appalachian Industrial School in Penland to serve as principal. Established in 1912, the school was founded by Reverend Rufus Morgan and funded by the Diocese of Western North Carolina. Students took regular school classes and learned to cook, take care of animals and work with clay, leather and paints. In 1924, Morgan established what became known as the Penland School of Crafts. She studied the craft movement at Berea College in Kentucky and brought ideas to the Toe River Valley. A cabin on the grounds of the school served as the first home of the Penland School. A 1928 article in *Handicrafter* introduced the school to the outside world, and letters began arriving from people across the nation, applying to study basketweaving, pottery, metalworking and silversmithing. Student crafts were the highlight

As it was at schools in Higgins and Crossnore, weaving was a lost skill taught at Penland. *University of North Carolina–Chapel Hill, Wilson Library Special Collections.*

Carding wool and spinning were demonstrated at the Penland School. *State Archives of North Carolina.*

Penland's original weaving cabin echoed an earlier time. *University of North Carolina–Chapel Hill, Wilson Library Special Collections.*

of the North Carolina exhibit at the Chicago World's Fair in 1933. Morgan continued to lead Penland School until 1962. Other programs were added over time, such as woodworking and glassblowing. By 2003, Penland School was annually drawing 1,200 students and 14,000 visitors to its 420-acre campus. While Penland's history is not well known across the country, it is a shining light in the Toe River Valley.[182]

Lucy Morgan passed away in July 1981 and is buried in Macon County. LeGette Blythe helped her write her 1958 autobiography, *Gift from the Hills: Miss Lucy Morgan's Story of Her Unique Penland School*. In 2007, a North Carolina Highway Historical Marker was placed on NC 226 denoting the importance of the Penland School.

Chapter 22

CROSSNORE SCHOOL'S HISTORY OF CARING FOR CHILDREN

By the early twentieth century, North Carolina public education had a state-mandated, tax-supported minimum four-month term. If enough money was not collected locally, school closed early. There were also no public high schools. High schools were funded by local communities and often by church denominations. It was into this world that Drs. Eustace and Mary Martin Sloop arrived along the North Toe River. Mary Martin was born in 1873 in Davidson, North Carolina, where her father taught geology and chemistry and served as interim president of Davidson College. She graduated from the Statesville Female College for Women and began her medical training at the North Carolina Medical College. Since women were not allowed to attend anatomy classes with male students there, she transferred to the Woman's Medical College of Pennsylvania, where she graduated; from there, she earned a postgraduate degree from Jefferson Medical School. She went on to become the first resident physician at Agnes Scott College in Georgia. Years earlier, she had met Eustace Sloop at Davidson College, and in 1908, they married. The Sloops moved to Plumtree, on the North Toe River, and for three years, they practiced medicine.[183]

Crossnore was a small community in the newly formed Avery County in 1911. There was a store, post office and a combination school and Baptist church. The Sloops soon integrated into local society, and Mary Sloop began advocating for better educational opportunities, opening a new school in 1913. Mary Sloop also began campaigning for a better life for

Crossnore School students learned to operate old looms, weaving textiles sold to support education. *State Archives of North Carolina.*

teenage girls, girls who often needed better clothes. Letters were sent and clothing donations arrived, which Sloop either gave to the young ladies or sold to provide money for suitable attire and funds necessary for the students to attend schools like Lees-McRae Institute and Berea College. Soon, the Sales Store opened, run by locals Aunt Pop and Uncle Gilmer, the proceeds funding scholarships, paying teacher salaries after the state-sponsored term expired and buying shop tools and sewing machines. Sloop soon had enough donations to build a teacherage, and local residents constructed a two-story building for vocational classes. In 1917, the General Assembly chartered Crossnore School Incorporated, which worked in tandem with the public school and provided religious and vocational education to students.[184]

With changes in state laws, construction began on a high school in 1918. The Altamont Consolidated High School graduated its first class in 1921. It was considered the best school in the county, and due to the number of students having to travel long distances, dormitories were constructed. Then came the dining hall. Classes were offered to adults as well as children. New teachers were educated at the school as well. In the mid-1920s, the attendance rate at other Avery County schools was 66 percent. At Crossnore, it was 96 percent. Then came the weaving room with looms, providing work that gave jobs to local women. And in 1928, a twenty-bed hospital opened. In 1937, work began on a new high school building. The money came from the Works Progress Administration, a part of the New Deal. A new elementary school soon followed. The high school building served the local population until 1968, when the three county high schools were consolidated into the new Avery County High School.[185]

Dr. Eustace Smith passed in 1961, and Mary Martin Sloop almost one year later, leaving an incredible legacy. She advocated for better schools, roads, medical care and agricultural practices. Thousands of children benefited from her tireless work. She was proclaimed North Carolina Mother of Year in 1951 and, later that same year, the "American Mother of the Year" by the Golden Rule Foundation. Working with LeGette Blythe, she published her autobiography, *Miracle in the Hills*, which won the Mayflower Cup award from the North Carolina Literary and Historical Association in 1953. Both Sloops are buried behind the church they helped build, Crossnore Presbyterian.[186]

Dr. Sloop, *far right*, inspects a trunk of clothing sent to help Crossnore School students. *Avery County Historical Museum.*

Crossnore School continues to thrive as Crossnore Communities for Children. The elementary school has moved, and the high school was torn down following county-wide consolidation. Crossnore Academy, now Williams Academy, opened in 1999. The school serves the children placed on the Crossnore Communities for Children campus and as a private school that community students can attend. The area continues to remember the contributions of the Sloops. Mary Sloop, the "Grand Lady of the Blue Ridge," is routinely included as one of the most influential people in Western North Carolina history. A section of U.S. Highway 221 was named as the Dr. Mary Martin Sloop Highway in 2006. Crossnore School has a North Carolina Highway Historical Marker, which was dedicated in 1997.[187]

Chapter 23

FAMOUS EXPLORERS AND COLOR WRITERS WHO VISITED THE TOE RIVER VALLEY

While isolated and seemingly forgotten by those in the General Assembly, the Toe River Valley of the eighteenth century was well known to naturalists. These botanists came to explore the rich diversity of the area, often leaving detailed descriptions of the places they visited and chronicling the area's hidden history in the process.

Frenchman André Michaux arrived around the time the area was being settled. Born at Satory, near Versailles, he was the son of a farmer on the king's estate. He eventually became a student of France's foremost botanist, Bernard de Jussieu. Later, Michaux studied the botany of Persia between 1782 and 1785. Michaux was then chosen to study the botany of North America, particularly the trees. Michaux arrived in New York in November 1785. He traveled the forests but also met the likes of Benjamin Franklin, Thomas Jefferson and William Bartram. In 1786, Michaux established a garden in Charleston, South Carolina. From there, he explored the mountains of southern Appalachia. In 1788, he passed through Charlotte, up the Catawba River and into the Blue Ridge area. He came back in 1794, following the well-worn road to the Bright Settlement and staying with Martin Davenport. On May 5, he "herborized in the vicinity of the dwellings of Davin Port and Wiseman," according to his journal. From there, he explored Roan and Yellow Mountains and the Toe River. On May 11, he climbed Humpback Mountain. He found rhododendrons, small-flowered lady's slipper, azaleas, lily of the valley and mayapple. By May 13, Michaux was moving up Bright's Trace into the present-day state of Tennessee. He returned in the summer

André Michaux, French naturalist and plant hunter, believed himself atop North America's highest peak after climbing Grandfather Mountain. *Wikicommons.*

Fraser firs, in the foreground, are named for botanist John Fraser. *Author's collection.*

of 1794, visiting the Black Mountains, Roan Mountain and Grandfather Mountain throughout the month of August. On Grandfather, Michaux thought he had reached the top of the highest mountain in North America. He sang the French national anthem and cried, "Long live America and the French Republic! Long live Liberty!"[188]

Scottish botanist John Fraser explored in the Roan Mountain area in 1787, 1789 and 1799. Like Michaux, he studied botany and explored widely. Fraser sailed with Captain James Cook, exploring the Australian coast in 1770. His early explorations of the New World in the 1780s were financed by the Linnean Society and then later by Russia's Catherine the Great. The Fraser fir, so common in southern Appalachia, is named for him.[189]

Also from Scotland was John Lyon. He was in Pennsylvania by 1796 and began collecting plants in 1799. Lyon was fond of both Roan and Grandfather Mountains. On a September 1808 visit to Roan Mountain, Lyon journaled that one storm lasted three days. He and his companions eventually made it off the mountain. Lyon described Roan Mountain as having "[in] general a fine rich soil with large growing trees of various sorts of Oaks, Walnuts, etc. which constitutes to a certain elevation or distance up the mountain when the same species suddenly assumes a more dwarf stunted appearance." Later, the trees disappeared and were replaced by a mix of shrubs that were difficult to navigate. Still higher up, the shrubs "altogether terminated. Then commences what the mountain people call the bald grounds," or grassy balds. The soils were "deep and rich producing fine grass and herbage more like that of natural meadows than mountains.… They will probably one day become the finest sheep pastures in the world." Lyon returned a year later and passed between Roan Mountain and Yellow Mountain at Carver's Gap. In the summer of 1812, he visited Roan, Yellow and Grandfather Mountains. Thirty-one new species are credited to Lyon. He passed away of tuberculous in Asheville in 1814.[190]

Dr. Elisha Mitchell, professor at the University of North Carolina, visited the area several times. In 1828, he wrote of touring Grandfather Mountain. After exploring the summit of the mountain, it was his group's plan to reach the cabin of Leatherstocking Aldridge "and feast upon Venison, Bear Meat and Honey." Darkness overtook them, and they were compelled to camp "on the top of Haw Ridge." Mitchell told his wife that if he were to come another summer, he would "locate myself on the Old Fields of Toe River and investigate the district lying between and around these high mountains." On an 1835 visit to Roan Mountain, Mitchell wrote that "with the exception of a body of (granite) rocks, looking like the ruins of an old castle, the top of Roan may be described as a vast meadow." Mitchell made repeated trips into the Black Mountains, one of which claimed his life in 1857.[191]

Asa Gray was the most famous botanist in America in the nineteenth century. Born in New York, Gray was a trained medical doctor who taught at Harvard University. He made several trips to the North Carolina mountains, beginning in 1841 when he visited Grandfather and Roan Mountains. Gray was looking for *Shortia galacifolia*, or Oconee bells, which were documented by André Michaux in 1794. Gray returned to the area in 1843, but he again failed to find the plant. Finally, in 1877, the Oconee bells were rediscovered, not in the Toe River Valley, but near Marion in McDowell County. Gray visited the area again in the spring of 1879 and last visited Roan Mountain in 1884.[192]

Asa Gray, nineteenth-century America's premier botanist, visited the Toe River Valley area several times. *Library of Congress.*

Quite possibly the most famous visitor came in 1885. John Muir was born in Scotland and immigrated to the United States with his family in 1849, settling in Wisconsin. After an injury working in an Indianapolis carriage workshop, Muir set out to see the world, walking to the Gulf of Mexico and sailing to Panama and then to California, where he made his home in the Sierra Nevada. In 1874, he began writing, drawing attention to the places he explored. In September 1898, Muir checked into the Cloudland Hotel on Roan Mountain. There he penned a letter to his wife, describing his trip from Cranberry and his hike along Roan Mountain. "All the landscapes in every direction are made up of mountains, a billowing sea of them without bounds as far as one can look," he wrote, "and every mountain hill and ridge and hollow is densely forested with so many kinds of trees their mere names would fill this sheet. & now they are beginning to put on their purple & gold." Muir spent a month roaming the mountains in the area. Often called the "father of our National Park System," Muir was personally involved in the creation of Yosemite, Sequoia, Mount Rainier, Petrified Forest and Grand Canyon National Parks.[193]

Travel writer Charles D. Warner, from Massachusetts, visited the Toe River Valley in 1888. Warner made stops in Banner Elk, Cranberry Forge, Roan, Bakersville and Burnsville. Big Tom Wilson convinced Warner that

John Muir visited in 1898, staying at Cloudland Hotel. *Library of Congress.*

a visit to the top of Mount Mitchell was worth the effort. It took five and a half hours to go from the Wilson residence to the peak. "What a magnificent forest!" Warner wrote. Then they reached the summit, which was "a nearly level spot of some thirty or forty feet….The stunted balsams have been cut away so as to give a view. The sweep of prospect is vast, and we could see the whole horizon….What we saw…was an inextricable tumble of mountains without order or leading line of direction-domes, peaks, ridges, endless and countless, everywhere, some in shadow, some tipped with shafts of sunlight, all wooded and green or black."[194]

Botanists, hikers and families from all over continue to explore the natural wonders of the Toe River Valley.

Chapter 24

WOMEN'S SUFFRAGE IN THE TOE RIVER VALLEY

bigail Adams, wife of John Adams, future president of the United States, requested that the founders, in drafting the Declaration of Independence, not put "unlimited power into the hands of husbands." Instead, they needed to "remember the ladies and be more generous and favorable to them than your ancestors." Alas, Adams and the other founding fathers did not remember the ladies when it came to electing officials. Voting was limited in most places to White and Black males who owned a certain amount of property. Free, property-owning Black men in North Carolina lost the right to vote during the Convention of 1835, when significant amendments were passed revising the 1776 constitution. Women remained largely forgotten in the political sphere.

Beginning in the mid-nineteenth century, small groups of women in various states began campaigning for causes, including temperance, antislavery and sundry moral reforms. A group meeting in 1848 in Seneca Falls, New York, declared that women had a right to vote. Black men across the nation gained the right to vote with the ratification of the Fifteenth Amendment in February 1870. A few months prior to the amendment's ratification, the National Woman Suffrage Association was formed. North Carolina was slow to join the fight. Many men and women felt that women should not be "marred" by the coarse, rough-and-tumble world of politics. In 1894, the North Carolina Equal Suffrage Association was formed in Asheville. Three years later, Republican state senator James Lee Hyatt from Burnsville introduced a bill in Raleigh "to provide for woman's suffrage in

North Carolina." It was February 1897, and the bill was referred to the committee on Insane Asylums. The bill died in committee.[195]

The idea that all citizens, male and female, should have the right to vote gained steam in the early part of the twentieth century. Several states passed laws allowing women to vote in local, statewide and presidential elections. North Carolina was not among them. Various groups in the state supported suffrage, and the Toe River Valley had its own voices in the fight. Mitchell County had the Bakersville Equal Suffrage Club, with Lillie Dale Lambert as president, Estelle Gudger as secretary and Birdie Prestwood as treasurer. Exactly how the Bakersville Equal Suffrage Club contributed to the actual suffrage debate is unknown, as are activities in Yancey County. In Avery County, sixty women gathered at the courthouse in Newland in October 1918 and passed resolutions urging Senator Lee S. Overman to support the passage of the Nineteenth Amendment that was then circulating. North Carolina governor Cameron Morrison was quoted in the *Raleigh News and Observer* as saying, "I am profoundly convinced that it would be part of wisdom and grace for North Carolina to accept the inevitable and ratify the amendment." However, it was not meant to be. On August 17, 1920, a motion was passed by the state senate postponing the ratification vote until the next legislative session. Two days later, the statehouse openly rejected ratification. North Carolina's actions were all in vain, for on August 21, the State of Tennessee claimed the honor of becoming the final state needed to ratify the constitutional amendment giving women the right to vote. North Carolina did not "get around" to ratifying the Nineteenth Amendment until 1971.[196]

A few women with Toe River connections were engaged in the national struggle for suffrage. Ella Clapp, born in Bakersville, was the daughter of local mica businessman Elisha B. Clapp. Ella married Edwin St. Clair Thompson in Washington, D.C., in 1908, and the couple lived in the city for a decade. While there, she became active in the woman's suffrage movement, serving as state field secretary for the Congressional Union and chairman of the National Women's Party in Spruce Pine. In March 1913, Thompson joined thousands of other women in a march for suffrage the

Bakersville native Ella St. Clair Thompson played an important role in the suffrage movement. *Library of Congress.*

day before Woodrow Wilson's presidential inauguration. Thompson spent months organizing groups in various communities across the United States and participated in various protests. She later studied law, and after her husband's death, she returned to North Carolina and practiced law until her death in 1944. Another woman active in the suffrage movement was Bulus Bagby Swift. She was not born in the area, only coming to the Montezuma community later in life. While living in Greensboro, she was a field worker for the North Carolina League of Women Voters and president of the North Carolina Congress of Parents and Teachers and worked with the Guilford County child welfare bureau during World War I. Following the passage of the Nineteenth Amendment, she worked on establishing an eight-hour workday and better educational standards. She, with her husband, Wiley Swift, moved to Montezuma in 1935, and both served as postmasters of the Montezuma Post Office. Bulus Swift passed away in 1952.[197]

While not everyone agreed, the right for women to vote was an important issue in the Toe River Valley, just as it was across the nation.

Chapter 25

A Few Famous People in the History of the Toe River Valley

Arizona Houston Hughes

Affectionately known as "Aunt Arizona," Arizona Houston Hughes (1876–1969) taught in local schools for fifty-seven years. Born on Henson's Creek in present-day Avery County, Aunt Arizona studied at the Wing School, then the Bowman Academy and finally the Fairview Collegiate Institute in Buncombe County. She then returned to Henson's Creek to teach, later teaching at schools in Peartree, Powder Mill, Yellow Mountain, Slippery Hill, Crabtree Creek and Roaring Creek. When school consolidation began in the 1930s, she transferred to Riverside Elementary. In 1953, she was honored as the North Carolina Teacher of the Year. Gloria Houston wrote an award-winning children's book about her life, *My Great-Aunt Arizona*.[198]

Big Tom Wilson

In an area well known for interesting characters, Big Tom Wilson (1825–1908) stands taller than most. A legendary hunter and guide, Wilson lived near the headwaters of the Cane River in Yancey County. He was often called to guide visitors through the Black Mountain range. It was Wilson who found Dr. Elisha Mitchell's body in 1857. After service as a Confederate musician during the Civil War, Wilson continued to hunt bears and guide. In 1895, he led the search party that found the body of naturalist John S.

"Aunt Arizona" Hughes was honored as the North Carolina Teacher of the Year. *Avery County Historical Museum.*

Cairns. At Wilson's passing, one newspaper wrote that "no man in western North Carolina was better known as a mighty huntsman than was Big Tom." Big Tom in the Black Mountains is named for him.[199]

SAM BENNETT

It is not easy being the last of anything, but Sam M. Bennett (1850–1951) was just that—the last of something. Bennett was North Carolina's last Civil War soldier. Lying about his age—he was only thirteen at the time, not sixteen—Bennett enlisted in the Confederate army, serving in the 58th North Carolina Troops. After being wounded, he spent the balance of the war serving as an orderly in a hospital. Bennett returned home to farm, marry and work as a blacksmith. In 1950, Bennett turned one hundred. He was interviewed by many, and his photograph even appeared in *LIFE* magazine. Sam Bennett passed on March 8, 1951. His death was covered across the South.[200]

HOWARD MARMON

Howard Marmon designed and built cars rivaling the best in the United States in the 1920s and 1930s. *Avery County Historical Museum.*

The Toe River Valley has attracted all sorts of people, from outlaws to entrepreneurs. Howard Marmon (1876–1943) was one of the entrepreneurs. Born in Indiana to an engineering family, after college he co-founded the Nordyke and Marmon Company, which produced its first car in 1902. Marmon later went on to establish the Marmon Motor Car Company, which eventually produced 250,000 automobiles, many of which rival the Cadillac and Peerless in quality. He held several patents, and many of his designs and features were revolutionary. Marmon built the Wasp, the car that won the first Indy 500. Like many of his class, he sought a respite in the mountains of Western North Carolina. As a boy, his family vacationed at the Cloudland Hotel and Eseeola. In the 1920s, he purchased the old Ritter Lumber Company community center in Pineola and had it renovated into a home, Hemlock Hedges. More than an absentee landowner who rarely visited, Marmon retired to the area. He established Anthony Lake Nursery, specializing in nature shrubbery, built a fish hatchery, was co-owner of the Kaolin Corporation in Ingalls and funded the construction of Pineola Presbyterian Church. Hemlock Hedges—which once played host to the likes of Henry Ford, Thomas Edison and Harvey Firestone—was razed early in the twenty-first century.[201]

LILI KRAUS

Budapest, Hungary, the birthplace of Lili Kraus (1903–1986), is far from the Toe River Valley. At the age of eight, Kraus entered Budapest's Royal Academy of Music and, at seventeen, the Vienna Conservatory of Music, later becoming a full professor at the school. In the 1930s, she toured Europe, married Otto Mandl, a German businessman, and moved to London, where they became naturalized British citizens. While touring in the Dutch East Indies in 1942, she was captured by the Japanese and spent three years as a prisoner of war. Following World War II, she resumed her career, traveling and playing piano recitals. In a series of concerts in New York, she played all twenty-five of Mozart's piano concertos. Kraus was considered the "First Lady of the Piano." She moved to Yancey County in 1969, while also serving as the artist-in-residence at Texas Christian University. Her last performance was in 1983.[202]

Lili Kraus, world-renowned concert pianist, retired to Yancey County and taught at Texas Christian University in the 1970s, pictured here. *Texas Christian University.*

TOMMY BURLESON

Seven feet, two inches tall is quite notable. Tommy Burleson (1952–), from Crossnore, Avery County, has often stood head and shoulders above just about everyone else. He was an All-American at both Newland High School and Avery County High School before heading off to play at North Carolina State University. While at NCSU, he helped the team win the 1974 NCAA Championship and was MVP of both the 1973 and 1974 ACC Tournaments. Burleson also played on the 1972 US Men's Olympic

Tommy Burleson played basketball for the 1972 Olympic Team and several professional teams. *Avery County Historical Museum.*

Basketball team in Munich, a team that lost a controversial gold medal game to the Soviet Union. The Americans refused to accept their silver medals. Burleson was also the last person to see the Israeli hostages before they were kidnapped. He entered the NBA draft in 1974, playing several seasons with the Seattle SuperSonics, Kansas City Kings and Atlanta Hawks. Retiring in 1981, Burleson returned to Avery County, raising a family and working in different ministries.[203]

LULU BELLE AND SCOTTY WISEMAN

Lulu Belle and Scotty Wiseman, mainstays at WLS in Chicago, performed all over the United States. *Avery County Historical Museum.*

Some of the most popular radio entertainers of the mid-twentieth century were born two counties apart. They had to go to Chicago to meet. Born in the Ingalls community of Mitchell County, Scotty Wiseman (1909–1981), grew up in a musical family in which nearly everyone played or sang. While attending college in West Virginia, he began to play on a local station. In 1932, he went to Chicago and became a regular on WLS, playing on the nationally syndicated *National Barn Dance.* Myrtle Cooper (1913–1999) was born in Boone and grew up in West Virginia. Her family moved to Chicago, and in 1932, she landed a job on WLS, performing under the stage name Lulu Belle, or "Belle of the Barn Dance." Her distinct style included a gingham dress, leather boots and braided hair. When Lulu Belle's onstage partner, Red Foley, married, she teamed up with Skyland Scotty. They were a comedy act, also singing love songs and traditional folk songs and ballads that Scotty had learned growing up along the North Toe River. In December 1935, the couple married and were soon billed as the Hayloft Sweethearts. In 1936, Lulu Belle was voted "National Radio Queen" by the subscribers of *Radio Guide.* The couple wrote numerous songs, including "Brown Mountain Lights," "Mountain Dew" and "Have I Told You Lately that I Love You?" In 1938, they were in Hollywood, costarring with Roy Rogers in *Shine On, Harvest Moon* and eventually working on seven different films. In 1958, the couple retired to the Ingalls community. Scotty earned a master's degree and began teaching. Lulu Belle served in the General Assembly from 1975 to 1978. They occasionally performed in Nashville, Renfro Valley and at Singing on the Mountain, and in 1969, they were honored with markers on the Country Music Hall of Fame's Walkway of Stars.[204]

SAM BRINKLEY

When the circus came to town, there were plenty of activities under the big tent. Not to be missed were the sideshows. Visitors could meet General Tom Thumb, only two feet, eight inches tall; Myrtle Corbin, the four-legged lady; Lionel the Lion Faced Man; or the man with the world's longest beard. That man was the Toe River Valley's own Sam Brinkley (1850–1929). While it took twenty years, his beard eventually reached the floor, an impressive feat since Brinkley was over six feet tall. He usually kept the beard rolled up in a bag, and for a dime, he would take it out and show it off. For several years he traveled with the Barnum & Bailey Circus as a part of the sideshow.[205]

Mitchell County's Sam Brinkley charged a dime to see his beard. *Claudia McGough.*

SHEPHERD MONROE DUGGER

Often called the "Grand Old Man of the Mountains," Shepherd Monroe Dugger (1854–1936) was one of the most important early writers in the three-county area. Born in Tennessee, Dugger moved to Banner Elk when he was two. He attended several colleges, including the University of North Carolina–Chapel Hill, before returning to the area to teach and serve as the first superintendent of Watauga County Schools. Undoubtedly, Dugger's greatest contributions were his articles and books. His articles appeared in numerous regional publications. *The Balsam Groves of the Grandfather Mountain*, written as an entry into a contest sponsored by the Linville Improvement Company, was released in 1892. Partly fictionalized, Dugger's book also included

Writer Shepherd Monroe Dugger promoted the history of the Toe River Valley. *Author's collection.*

parts of the journals of André Michaux and Elisha Mitchell, along with a "Dictionary of Altitudes." In 1932, Dugger published *War Trails of the Blue Ridge*. This tome contains histories of the Battle of Kings Mountain, the Civil War skirmish on Beech Mountain and Kirk's Raid on Camp Vance, as well as histories of Avery County, Linville and Banner Elk.[206]

Gloria Houston

Growing up in the Toe River Valley with a father who was one of the old collectors of story and history provided inspiration to Gloria Houston (1941–2016). Myron Houston collected and preserved much history in lower Avery and Mitchell Counties. Gloria grew up steeped in that history before earning degrees from Appalachian State University and the University of South Florida. She considered herself primarily a teacher and penned ten books that sold millions of copies. Frequently, she wrote about the Toe River Valley and her family. *My Great Aunt-Arizona* was about her aunt, Arizona Houston, who taught for more than fifty years. *The Year of the Perfect Christmas Tree* tells the story of a young girl during World War I. It was a *Publishers Weekly* best-seller and named Best Book of the Decade by the American Library Association. Many remember Gloria Houston fondly, as she brought the Toe River area to many in her children's books.[207]

Charlie McKinney

The "Forty Charlie" or "Cove Charlie" are not nicknames that have a catchy ring. Yet they appropriately describe the life of Charles "Charlie" McKinney (1780–1858). As the story goes, Charlie McKinney was born in Scotland, moved to Grassy Creek in present-day Mitchell County and finally relocated to present-day Burke County. McKinney brought with him apple seeds, planting orchards. He also had four wives, all at once, and up to forty-eight children. Those wives were Elizabeth Lowery, Margaret "Peggy" Lowery, Sarah "Sally" Hopson and Nancy Triplett. There are numerous local stories about the families—how they all went to church together and loaded up to go to town to buy necessities. Even if parts of Charlie's story are the stuff of legend, many people in the Toe River Valley are related to one another, tracing their heritage to Charlie McKinney.[208]

Lesley Riddle

The mountains and hollers of the Toe River Valley have a rich history of music and musicians. One of those celebrated artists was Lesley Riddle (1905–1980). Born in Burnsville, he learned to play guitar while recovering from an accident. Around 1928, Riddle met A.P. Carter. Impressed with

Riddle's playing, Carter invited Riddle to travel with him collecting songs. Riddle also helped teach several songs to Maybelle Carter. After moving to New York in 1937, Riddle no longer played. During the folk revival of the 1960s, Mike Seeger sought out Riddle and convinced him to begin playing again. Riddle played at numerous folk festivals and recorded several songs that were released after his death. There is a North Carolina Historical Marker dedicated to this important African American musician.[209]

JESSE STATON

Born near Bakersville in May 1895, Jesse Staton moved to the Cranberry area prior to September 1917. On September 19, 1917, he enlisted to go fight in what became known as the Great War, or the War to End All Wars. Staton served in Company M, 321st Infantry Regiment, 81st Division, and arrived in France on August 13, 1918. November 11 was the first big battle for his regiment. They were up and over the trenches near Grimscourt early that morning, charging the Germans, when Staton was struck in the chest by shell fragments. A few hours later that same day, the armistice went into effect, ending the war. Staton was one of 2,738 killed the last day of the war. His remains were returned to the United States in May 1921 and interred at the Cranberry Cemetery.[210]

CHARLES W. RAY

Charles Woodfin Ray was born on August 6, 1872, in the Pensacola community. The son of Hiram and Rachel McPeters Ray, Charles enlisted in the army in 1898, eventually making sergeant in Company I, 22nd U.S. Infantry. Sergeant Ray was leading a detachment from his company. As they approached a bridge near San Isidro, Luzon, Philippine Islands, he noticed that the planks had been removed to slow their advance. Ray led a charge, attempting to cross the bridge on the stringers. They were able to hold the bridge, allowing the rest of his regiment to advance and cross. Ray had a bout with malaria and, after recovering, was making his way back to his company when he was attacked and kidnapped by insurgents. This resulted in the loss of his left arm above the elbow. In 1902, Ray was awarded the Medal of Honor for his actions. Upon returning home, Ray married Myrtle Louis. The couple eventually had eight children and made their way to Oklahoma. When Ray passed in 1959, he was one of the oldest Medal of Honor awardees alive in the United States. Ray is the only Medal of Honor winner from the Toe River Valley.[211]

Chapter 26

HAIL TO THE HIDDEN HISTORY OF PRESIDENTIAL VISITS

At one time, presidents of the United States made sweeping journeys through parts of the country via horse and buggy and, later, railroads. In other parts of the state, signs often declare that George Washington visited a particular place on his 1791 trip through the South. While Washington never slept in the Toe River Valley, there have been a few other commanders in chief who have visited the jewel of the Blue Ridge.

Andrew Jackson might have been the first with future ties to the presidency to set foot in the Toe River Valley. Born near Waxhaw, on the North Carolina/South Carolina border in 1767, Jackson was the only member of his family to survive the American Revolution. Following the war, Jackson made the trip to Burke County, asking Waightstill Avery to take him on as a law student. Avery turned him down, and Jackson studied law in Salisbury. In 1786 or 1787, Jackson was admitted to the bar. He practiced law on the frontier, trying his first case in Jonesborough (now Tennessee) in August 1788. Opposing counsel at the trial was none other than Waightstill Avery. He and Jackson undoubtedly traveled along the old Bright's Trace from Morganton, along the North Toe River, up Roaring Creek and across Roan Mountain. Avery and Jackson had a failing out at a trial in Jonesborough in which Jackson challenged the senior statesman to a duel. There are two different accounts about what happened at the duel outside Jonesborough. One account has both men firing into the air, while another has Jackson firing and missing and Avery refusing to fire, giving Jackson a lecture instead.

Vice President Richard M. Nixon visited Mitchell and Avery Counties in June 1958, speaking at the Roan Mountain Rhododendron Festival. *Hugh Morton/Grandfather Mountain.*

Avery died in 1821, and Jackson went on to serve in the U.S. House, U.S. Senate, as a judge and as major general of the Tennessee militia, all before becoming president of the United States.[212]

Andrew Johnson probably took the same route along the North Toe River. Johnson, born in Raleigh in 1808, ran away from his apprenticeship and in 1826 moved to Greeneville, Tennessee. Johnson later became mayor of Greeneville, served in the U.S. House, served as governor of Tennessee and served in the U.S. Senate before ascending to the presidency upon the assassination of Abraham Lincoln in April 1865. Not widely popular and often incurring the wrath of the radical Republicans, Johnson was the first president to be impeached, although he escaped conviction by one vote. He passed away in Carter County, Tennessee, in 1875.[213]

Theodore Roosevelt might have visited the Toe River Valley. Roosevelt, born in New York in 1858, served as president between 1901 and 1909. He made several visits to North Carolina, both as president and when he chose to run again in 1912. In 1902, he came as close as Old Fort when a train carrying him from Asheville east stopped to take on water. Roosevelt supposedly accepted an invitation from J.S. Penland of Linville Falls to bear hunt in the area in December 1904, but details of the trip are lacking. Roosevelt was again in North Carolina in 1905, and in 1912, while running for a third term, he traveled again via rail from Asheville through Salisbury to Greensboro. However, although there is an image of Roosevelt supposedly taken at a mine in the Toe River Valley, it is difficult to pinpoint just when this image was taken. Roosevelt lost to William H. Taft and died in 1919.[214]

Richard Nixon did not visit the area once he became president but did travel here when he was vice president. On June 21, 1958, Nixon made a quick tour of several local places. He visited Roan Mountain, Bakersville and Spruce Pine and then came to Banner Elk, where he turned a shovelful of dirt at the groundbreaking of the new Grace Hartley Memorial Hospital. The crowd on Roan Mountain was estimated to be ten thousand. Nixon

Gerald Ford spoke in the rain at Morrison Field at the Avery County Airport in March 1976. *Gerald Ford Library.*

spoke on the importance of the American Revolution. In Spruce Pine, he was given a key to the city that was made of local "high grade ruby mica." After Banner Elk, the vice president and his wife headed to Blowing Rock. Nixon served as president from 1969 to 1974 and passed away in 1994.[215]

Gerald Ford paid a special visit to Avery County on March 20, 1976. Ford, the thirty-eighth president of the United States, was supposed to have flown via helicopter from Asheville to Morrison Field in Avery County for a rally. Fog prevented flying. Instead, a presidential motorcade brought President Ford, along with Governor James Holshouser, to Avery County for the rally. When canceling the trip was mentioned to Ford, he reportedly said, "The people are waiting in the rain, and I promised that I would be there." Charles L. Buchanan, mayor of Spruce Pine and Charles B. Von Cannon, mayor of Banner Elk, greeted the president. President Ford addressed the crowd for about thirteen minutes before being whisked away to Hickory. Ford passed away in 2006.

There have probably been a few other visits over the years. Jimmy Carter reportedly stayed at the Nu-Wray Inn in Burnsville, and Barack Obama rode a bus through Banner Elk on his way to a rally in Boone. Many others probably slipped quietly in and out of the Toe River Valley on their personal and presidential journeys.

Chapter 27

LOST HOSPITALS OF THE
TOE RIVER VALLEY

Hospitals and medical centers abound in the Toe River Valley in
the twenty-first century. Thanks to good roads, services unavailable
locally are just a short drive away in Boone or Asheville. That
was not always the case. For more than the first one hundred years after
European settlement in the Toe River Valley, medical services were limited
to a handful of doctors and granny women or root doctors.

Most families who settled in the area in the late 1700s had some
rudimentary medical knowledge. They understood what roots, barks and
leaves could be harvested for their medical properties. Ginger, blackberry
leaves and roots, elderberries and echinacea were all native and are still in
use today. Settlers would have brought some medical knowledge with them
when they arrived and learned more from traders who had interacted with
the Shawnees, Catawbas and Cherokees. Quite possibly the area's first
doctor with more formal training was Ebenezer Childs. Dr. Childs probably
studied under his father, also a doctor, in Shelburne, Massachusetts, and was
reported as having "obtained great eminence as a physician." Childs moved
his family to the North Toe River, settling near the old Bright settlement
and opening a post office. This, of course, was the site of Childsville, later
Calhoun, the first county seat for Mitchell County. Dr. Childs died in 1862.
Another formally trained doctor was Benjamin B. Whittington, who studied
at the medical college in Charleston, South Carolina. Several others arrived
prior to the 1860s, but their levels of training seem lost to history.[216]

The medical practices of these early doctors followed a similar pattern. A doctor would move into a community and set up an office, possibly a room in his home. Most of his practice, however, was done via a horse or horse and buggy. A call might arrive at any hour day or night, and the doctor would saddle his horse, gather his bag with instruments and medicines and set out to the patient's location. Patient visiting occurred in every type of weather, and there were always numerous rivers and creeks to cross. Mary Martin Sloop recalled one night having to take a hammer to Dr. Sloop's boots, busting the ice so he could get his feet out of the stirrups. Doctors were sometimes paid with cash, but just as often with produce or poultry. Dentist William W. Whittington of Yancey County recalled going to see a woman with an "earache, who lived way up on the side of a mountain." After traversing "deep snow," Whittington found that she had a "severe mastoid infection." Without instruments or chloroform, he felt he had to do something. "She drank about a pint of whiskey, and was soon drunk as a fool. I slipped the point of ordinary scissors under the skin and bored a hole until I reached the infection site. Lots of pus ran out." A week later, the woman was well. "I was paid in corn, which I hauled to town and sold for 75 cents." Usually, a healthy member of the family, at times a youngster, was sent for the doctor. One family in Kona wrote to their doctor when the doctor's services were needed, placing the letter in the mail bag picked up by the train. The doctor would arrive two or three days later. This remained the norm into the early twentieth century, even after the advent of automobiles, better roads and hospitals.[217]

The first documented mention of a hospital in the area comes during the Civil War. A hospital for those afflicted with smallpox was set up in the Pensacola area. It could be that a type of county home already existed there under the direction of Nathan Ray and that smallpox victims were assigned to his care. While there were a few hospitals in large cities prior to the war, it was the war itself that provided many men with experience in institutional healthcare facilities. Prior to this time, hospitals were seen as places for indigent people. Many men wound up in hospitals during the war, being treated for sickness or wounds. Following the war, hospitals as institutions for everyone slowly began to come of age, although it took time for the concept to make its way to rural areas.[218]

Avery County

A growing population in the Toe River Valley brought the need for better medical practitioners. Companies like the Cranberry Iron Mines and some lumber mills had company doctors or nurses that established offices in the camps. Some of the larger hotels also employed a staff physician during the peak summer months. It took a Presbyterian missionary to get the hospital ball rolling. Edgar Tufts was sent to Banner Elk to plant a church. He founded not only a church but also an orphanage and hospital. In 1908, Tufts had raised enough funds to build a fourteen-room hospital and physician's home on the campus of Lees-McRae Institute. Charles Reed was the first physician. Two of the rooms had beds for patients, while others contained an office, examination room and laboratory for compounding medicine. Dr. Reed only stayed a few years before relocating and being replaced by a recent medical school graduate, William M. Tate. Dr. Tate was working at a lumber camp in Pineola when Tufts persuaded him to come to Banner Elk. He opened more rooms to patients and began to work on a surgical room. A nurse was brought on staff in 1914. The hospital became known as Grace Hospital, named for one of the hospital's benefactor's sisters. In 1924, Grace Hospital II opened. The new brick hospital had twenty beds, along with a waiting room, pathology lab, X-ray equipment, operating room and living quarters for nurses. The hospital employed twenty-two, including a new physician, Dr. R.H. Hardin. Grace Hospital II only lasted a decade. The facility, one of the leading hospitals in the western part of North Carolina, became overcrowded. Grace Hospital III, completed in 1932, contained sixty patient beds. Like the previous Grace Hospitals, this one was located on the grounds of Lees-McRae College. The old Grace Hospital II became a nursing school, with classrooms and a dormitory. The official name of the new facility was the Grace Hartley Memorial Hospital, and it officially opened in May 1932. Dr. Hardin died in 1937 and was replaced by several others, including Dr. James Brown and Dr. Clifford Seaman. This hospital served for many years until the need for a new facility became evident. Groundbreaking for the new facility was held on June 21, 1958. Vice President Richard M. Nixon turned the first shovelful of dirt. The new one-hundred-bed facility would not carry the name of Grace. There was actually a Grace Hospital in Morganton. Instead, the hospital was named the Charles A. Cannon Jr. Memorial Hospital. Cannon was a pilot killed in World War II, and his family members were benefactors for the new structure. The new Cannon Hospital opened for patients on January 25, 1961. Grace Hospital

The campus of Lees-McRae College in Banner Elk has had three Grace Hospitals, including Grace Hospital III. *Author's collection.*

III became Tate dorm at Lees-McRae. Dr. Tate passed away in 1984. Many people were surprised to hear that plans were underway to build yet another new hospital in Avery County. However, the high cost of maintaining two hospitals in one county led to the creation of a new, centrally located facility consolidating the Banner Elk and Crossnore hospitals. The new Cannon Hospital in Linville opened in December 1999. As of 2023, the first Cannon Hospital sits abandoned.[219]

About the time that Tufts was working on building a hospital in Banner Elk, a couple, both doctors, were working on a medical facility in Crossnore. Mary Martin Sloop and Eustace Sloop were both university-trained doctors. From the Piedmont section of North Carolina, they settled in Plumtree, working as doctors for the Plumtree School for Boys. For several reasons, they chose in 1911 to relocate to the Crossnore community. At first, they had an office at home, while Eustace Sloop made house calls. Thanks to the Duke Endowment, Garrett Memorial Hospital opened in 1928. The stone building had twenty-two beds for patients, ten bassinets, a doctor's office and X-ray room, all on the main floor. The upstairs housed sleeping quarters for "student aides." For the next ten years, Crossnore had one doctor and, for twenty years, one registered nurse. Instead of tearing down and rebuilding, or building on a new site, Garrett Memorial Hospital just expanded. A new wing housing thirty-eight beds came in 1972. Intensive and coronary care facilities were added in 1976. Then came a dining hall and offices for the doctors. Eustace Sloop passed away in February 1961. The name of the hospital was changed from Garrett Memorial to Sloop Memorial. The hospital closed in 1999, consolidated with the hospital in Banner Elk to form the new Cannon Memorial Hospital in Linville. The building housing doctors' offices at Cannon is named the Sloop Medical Plaza, and there is a display about the two hospitals in the lobby. In the twenty-first century, the additions to the Crossnore hospital were demolished, leaving the original building, which was restored, refurbished and is now used as offices by the Crossnore Communities for Children.[220]

MITCHELL COUNTY

Like the Avery County area, Mitchell County had several doctors who opened small offices but who spent a great deal of time riding the hills and valleys attending sick patients. Sick community members often tried home remedies before calling a professional doctor. When the doctor arrived, the sick were frequently in dangerous circumstances. Some of those late nineteenth- and early twentieth-century doctors include Virgil R. Butt, A.E. Gouge, J.B. Ewing and C.E. Smith. As in Avery and Yancey Counties, a multitude of midwives delivered babies in the communities where they resided. Lydia Holman came first as a private nurse, licensed by the state in 1905, and then returned to establish a health and welfare center on fifteen acres provided by the Holston Land Company in Altapass. Holman's clinic, sometimes referred to as the Holman Hospital, made national news. The Philadelphia-trained nurse and Spanish-American War veteran was considered an "American Florence Nightingale." According to one newspaper, Holman brought medical care to "forgotten mountaineers and backwoodsmen," fighting "many local prejudices and local selfishness." Holman was given property, an old hospital building constructed by the Clinchfield Railroad construction crew, to repurpose as her new facility. She went on to organize the Holman Association for the Promotion of Rural Nursing, Hygiene and Social Service. The organization, founded in 1910, had a national board, and Holman spent some time traveling to raise funds for her hospital and to advocate for better healthcare for rural America. According to one account, Holman petitioned President Herbert Hoover, asking for a car so she could reach the sick more easily. Hoover replied to the request, and Holman could be seen traveling about in a car she called the "Hoovermobile." Feller Lowery was her driver. Holman did great work in the surrounding communities. However, her depiction of local mountaineers as living in log houses with no windows, not knowing that there was a federal government and of children having to share clothes and being taught to use tobacco at an early age brought pushback and resentment from locals. Holman's claims that there were "no medical men within hundreds of miles[;]...people are the prey of herb doctors, quacks and charlatans" angered one local. He responded with a letter to a Raleigh newspaper, stating that within five miles of Holman's home were five licensed physicians, graduates of some of the best medical schools in the country. The author of the letter, Dr. J.B. Ewing, noted that Holman "forgot to mention the fact that she was indicted for practicing medicine without a license and the case was nolle-prossed on her promise to quit the practice and to confine her activities to her profession as a nurse." Holman continued to nurse and educate local people on health. Her hospital operated for thirty years, and then later, she opened a library. She passed away in 1960 and is buried in Spruce Pine.[221]

Several doctors set up practice in Spruce Pine in the first few decades of the twentieth century. Charles A. Peterson, Critz F. Lambert and L.L. Williams all had offices or clinics within town limits. On January 7, 1930, the board of aldermen of the town of Spruce Pine adopted an ordinance authorizing the issue of bonds for a new hospital. In March 1930, the citizens of Spruce

The first Holman Hospital in Altapass was built by the Clinchfield Railroad construction crew. *From the* Visiting Nurse Quarterly *(1912).*

Pine voted to issue $35,000 in bonds, matching a Duke Foundation Grant for a new hospital, aptly named Duke Municipal Hospital. The proposed hospital ran into serious opposition. Some believed that the hospital would not be self-supporting and that the additional tax on people would be unbearable. Several community members sued the town but lost when the case was argued before the state Supreme Court. In March 1931, a bill was introduced in the statehouse that would allow the bonds to be delivered and sold. The bill passed the House but was tabled in the Senate. It was not until 1955 that the Spruce Pine Community Hospital opened. Like the hospitals in Banner Elk and Crossnore, part of the funds for this new hospital were provided through a Duke Endowment. The project was led by the Junior Women's Club of Spruce Pine and cost $400,000. As of this writing, the Spruce Pine Community Hospital is now a part of the Blue Ridge Regional Hospital—a part of the Mission Health/HCA System.[222]

Bakersville was not without medical offices. Dr. Robert Prestwood built the first freestanding medical office and pharmacy in Mitchell County prior to 1899. The building now survives as the Mitchell County Historical Museum. Paul McBee ran the McBee Clinic in the 1930s. Dr. A.E. Gouge built an office next to his home in 1934. He did not retire until 1964. The McBee Clinic was reopened as the Dorothy Carolyn Hospital in 1949. This facility had six beds and four bassinets. This facility closed in the late 1950s. Dr. George Kimberly came to Bakersville in 1960, opening an office in a second-story building. Later, he built an office that he shared with Dr. J.T. McRae. However, neither stayed through the end of the decade. In November 1974, the building was opened as the Bakersville Community Medical Clinic. Governor James Holshouser spoke at the dedication. As of 2023, the clinic survives as the Mountain Community Health Partnership.[223]

Yancey County

Yancey County, the parent county to Mitchell and Avery, had its fair share of early doctors and midwives, available pretty much any time of day or night. An 1890 business directory reported six doctors in Burnsville alone: W.M. Austin, J.M. Fairchilds, Thomas Houston, O.M. Lewis, J.L. Ray and W.P. Whittington. B.B. Whittington was listed in Cane River, and L. Whittington was in Day Book. Traditional health clinics and hospitals were slow to arrive. Dr. E.R. Ohle was born in Germany, immigrated to the United States in 1934, graduated from Harvard Medical School in 1941 and, following an internship at Yale University, moved to Yancey County. By early 1946, Ohle was serving as the resident physician of the Celo Cooperative Community. Later that year, Ohle became the staff doctor of the other medical facility in Yancey County, the Higgins Clinic. The clinic was a part of the Higgins Neighborhood Center Inc., a mission project of the Presbyterian Church (North). A clinic in Celo was opened in 1946 or 1947. The clinic in Celo continues to see patients through 2023.[224]

There had been talk of a hospital in Burnsville as early as 1928. The Duke Foundation had pledged $10,000, and local citizens were debating a $30,000 bond issue to fund the project, which apparently passed. A bill was introduced in the General Assembly to appoint trustees in 1929. The bill passed the House but apparently failed in the Senate. An effort to construct a hospital in Burnsville was reborn in the 1950s. The hospital was a twenty-two-bed facility and had a projected cost of $100,000, although some of the labor was provided by volunteers. Work began in June 1952, and the dedication was held on September 6, 1953. A new hospital was built in 1976, and the old hospital became the offices for the Yancey County Health Department. The new hospital, a part of the Blue Ridge Hospital System, closed in 1992 and was reborn as the Yancey Community Medical Center. Now, it is known as the Blue Ridge Medical Center–Yancey Campus, a part of Mission Health/HCA.[225]

Chapter 28

HISTORIC NATURAL DISASTERS

Floods, fires, famines, earthquakes and epic snowstorms are all a part of Toe River Valley history, history that is sometimes hidden or wiped away. There are a few nineteenth-century events that were witnessed, or felt, by local residents, like the New Madrid Earthquakes in 1811–12 and the "Night the Stars Fell" in November 1833. Those occurrences early in Toe River Valley history garnered far less attention than events in the twentieth century.

FLOODS

While localized freshets are frequent occurrences, there have been several devastating floods in the Toe River Valley. At the end of May 1901, it was reported that the "Toe river is out of all bounds." The railroad was "completely washed away in many places." Several barns and houses in Yancey County were demolished. The Baptist church in Bakersville was destroyed, just one of twenty-four buildings completely obliterated. Fifteen years later, another serious flood hit the area. A storm formed in the Gulf of Mexico and moved up through the South, stalling along the Blue Ridge Mountains. Rain began to fall on July 5, 1916, and it rained for six days. While this storm saturated the grounds in the mountains, a second "tropical cyclone" formed off the Atlantic Ocean and moved into South Carolina on the morning of July 14. This storm moved quickly, and the center was over Western North Carolina by the morning of July 15. The rain began in

Flood damage can be seen at Mile Marker 305, Blue Ridge Parkway, August 1940. *State Archives of North Carolina.*

earnest on Saturday morning, July 16. Altapass reported receiving more than twenty-two inches of rain in a twenty-four-hour period, a record that has yet to be broken in North Carolina. This much rain produced flooding that destroyed homes and businesses, while also washing out railroad trackage for the Clinchfield, the ET&WNC and the LRR. The iron bridge over the North Toe River in Spruce Pine was washed away. Numerous landslides were reported in places like Linville and on Mount Mitchell. Several lives were lost. The "Second Great Flood" began in August 1940. On August 11, a hurricane came ashore in South Carolina and quickly worked its way west. As there had already been an abundance of rain that month, many streams were quickly out of their banks. Once again, the railroads were wrecked. The LRR was never rebuilt. Roads between communities were closed due to landslides. One newspaper reported that every highway in Yancey County was greatly damaged. Lumber and sawmills were washed away and crops severely damaged. The Red Cross was sent to various communities to help with disaster relief. One other flood of the twentieth century bears mention. On November 4, 1977, heavy rain began to fall in the area. Two days later, up to eleven inches were reported in some places. Several roads were washed out, and there were landslides in Glen Ayre and Loafer's Glory. This was the flood that destroyed many of the newspapers in Yancey County and school records in Mitchell County. Sixteen different counties in Western North Carolina were designated national disaster areas.[226]

SNOW

Snow is a common occurrence most winters in the Toe River Valley. There have been a few snowstorms in the past one hundred years that have been truly memorable. The winter of 1936 was extremely cold, and by early March, the mercury had dipped more than ten degrees below zero several times. Sometime around March 18–19, snow commenced falling and blowing. At the end of the storm, Mount Mitchell reported twenty-one inches. Hundreds of school-age children were left stranded in their Newland school, with drifts up to twenty feet. Local citizens dug through the snow and provided children with food, bedding and additional warm garments. Many children were moved to private houses in town. It took days for their parents to arrive and escort the students to their snow-covered homes. The winter of 1959–60 was another for the record books. Snow was reported on January 7 and January 21, and then on February 13, it began snowing every Monday, continuing until March 26. More than eighty-three inches of snow were reported. The governor ordered a state of emergency, and the North Carolina National Guard dropped food, fuel and medical supplies to stranded families. It took a long time for the snow to melt and schools to reopen. One final snowstorm deserves mention: the Blizzard of 1993. On

The Toe River Valley has had numerous blizzards, like this 1936 Newland one. *Avery County Historical Museum.*

March 13, snow blanketed the area. Accumulations on Mount Mitchell were estimated at three feet, with drifts much higher. At least the same amount—three feet—fell in Bakersville. Schools were canceled for more than a week. Drifts on Roan Mountain were reported up to ten feet high. Many people lost power due to the high winds.[227]

EARTHQUAKES

While earthquakes in our area are fairly rare, they do occasionally occur. Local residents undoubtedly felt the New Madrid Earthquakes in 1811–12 and the earthquake in Charleston, South Carolina, in August 1886. More localized earthquakes include one in August 1895, during which Shepherd M. Dugger reported from the Banner Elk community that "the kitchen furniture jingled severely, and a pile of fence rails was shaken down, in the presence of some men who were making hay." In July 1926, a reported 5.2 magnitude earthquake in Mitchell County brought state geologist Dr. Collier Cobb to Toecane, investigating a quake that had taken place the previous week. The geologist found cracked foundations and chimneys, and at least one water pipeline was broken. A "sharp shock" in Burnsville accompanied a quake in May 1957. It was also felt in Newland and Spruce Pine. While the fault lines in California get plenty of attention, it might come as a surprise to learn that one also runs through Avery, Mitchell and Yancey Counties.[228]

FIRES

Fires are nothing new to the area. Often started by lightning and, later, by careless individuals or even steam locomotives, they are not the cataclysmic events so often viewed in the western states. A few of the more devastating fires include one in Elk Park in December 1903 that destroyed much of the town's business district; an October 1923 fire in Bakersville that destroyed two blocks of businesses and several homes; a January 1941 fire in Newland that destroyed seven businesses; and a January 1961 fire in Newland that took out two blocks of businesses. These early fires led to towns and communities investing in firefighting equipment and the establishment of various firefighting stations, staffed primarily by volunteer firefighters.[229]

Chapter 29

TOE RIVER VALLEY HISTORY SHORTS

W hile many of the history tales hidden in the Toe River Valley are quite detailed and others are part of a connected history, some of these hidden gems are just little snapshots of the past.

CANE RIVER NATIVE AMERICAN SITE

When construction workers began digging a ditch for a new sewer line at Cane River Middle School in Yancey County in July 1989, they uncovered a Native American burial. The discovery brought a stop to the trench and a call to the North Carolina State Archaeological Office. The archaeologist determined that there was a Native American village at the site, dating from AD 1000 to AD 1500. For four weeks, parts of the centuries-old village were excavated. Archaeologists concluded that the site, four to five acres in size, contained a palisaded village that included square-shaped houses and pits for cooking and food storage. Four burials were found, one of which was removed for study and then returned to the site. Also found were numerous pot shards, vessels and points. The artifacts are housed at the Rush Wray Museum in Burnsville.

Lost Garland Silver Mine

There are tales of lost mines and hidden treasures in almost every community. The most famous in Appalachia is the story of the lost Swift Silver Mines. Swift's mine was probably located in eastern Kentucky but had some North Carolina ties. John Swift, who originally found the mine, lived in North Carolina, and on a trip back from Kentucky, he supposedly hid part of that treasure in the Elk Park Falls area. There is another treasure/mine shaft a little closer to the Toe River Valley: the Lost Garland Silver Mine. This one is located in the Unaka Mountains, a range that separates North Carolina from Tennessee along the north border of the Toe River Valley. The story goes like this: William Garland was out bear hunting one day. As he was crawling through the laurel to find his dogs, he discovered a mine. Garland picked up a few rocks that "later proved to be to be silver and lead." He returned to the mine several times throughout his life, packing out the silver. Once, he took his son Charles to the mine, but Charles could never find it again. William Garland probably died in 1871, and while countless people have searched the Unaka Mountains, no one has ever located the Lost Garland Silver Mine.[230]

Smithsonian Solar Observatory

Hump Mountain, above Elk Park, seems an unlikely place for a bit of hidden history. Yet in 1917, the Smithsonian Institute chose to place an astrophysical observatory there. The solar observatory was scheduled to go to Chile, but World War I intervened. Property was leased from Huff Brothers and Reynolds, and two buildings were constructed. One building housed the observatory, while the other was living quarters. The instruments, hauled in on the ET&WNC, were to take "measures of the solar constant of radiation, measures of the brightness of the sky, measures of nocturnal radiation, and experiments bearing on frost prediction." The observers worked for almost a year, although some of the instruments were sent away to be repaired. In the end, it was often too cloudy to get good readings. By the summer of 1918, the equipment was on its way to Chile.[231]

World War II Radio Tower on Mount Mitchell

While people often think that World War II was "over there," it was in the Toe River Valley as well. Local mica had a direct impact on the war. Aircraft Warning Service posts, staffed by volunteers, dotted the area. Victory Gardens were grown, scrap drives took place, Victory Bonds were bought and the National Youth Administration trained local young people in skills like welding, sewing and machining. Crossnore School manufactured wooden airplanes used in pilot training. On Mount Mitchell, troops were stationed at the studio/transmitter for W41MM, and a bunker was built for the staff in case of attack. It was feared that the station could be seized by enemy operatives and used to transmit subversive propaganda. The signal from the radio station was so strong that German U-boats could pick it up after surfacing off the North Carolina coast, allowing them to pinpoint their location.[232]

Hale Telescope at the Palomar Observatory

At the time it was constructed, the two-hundred-inch Hale Telescope at the Palomar Observatory in San Diego County, California, was the largest telescope in the world. The telescope was built by George E. Hale and first used by Edwin Hubble in January 1949. What does a telescope in

The Hale Telescope at the Palomar Observatory near San Diego, California, is constructed of Mitchell County quartz. *Author's collection.*

California have to do with the Toe River Valley? Actually, quite a bit. The quartz for the mirror in the Hale Telescope was mined at the Chestnut Flat Mine in Ledger, Mitchell County. In 1934, after being closely inspected for any flaws, four boxcars' worth of Toe River Valley quartz were loaded onto a Clinchfield train and first transported to Consolidated Feldspar Corporation in Erwin, Tennessee, to be ground into a fine mesh. The quartz was shipped to the Corning Glass Works in New York, where it was poured into a mold and heated to 2,400 degrees Fahrenheit. The heating process fused the quartz into the large mirror. It took a year for the nearly fifteen-ton mirror to cool. World War II delayed the installation of the mirror until 1948. The Hale Telescope was the largest in the world until 1976 and the second largest until 1993. It is still used in research, with the quartz mirror from Mitchell County.[233]

LOCAL SAND ON GOLF COURSES ACROSS THE COUNTRY

There are several golf courses in the Toe River Valley, both public and private. But even golf courses far from the Toe River may have a bit of the area as part of their landscape. Golfers at Augusta National Golf Club in Georgia are playing on a piece of the Toe River Valley. The "sand" in the traps at Augusta is actually SP55, an igneous sand made up of granulated quartz mined in Mitchell County. The igneous sand is a waste byproduct of the quartz industry. In the 1970s, Augusta's chief executive, Clifford Roberts, began searching for an alternative for the sand traps. Roberts had a seasonal home in Avery County and knew that the Linville Golf Club used the sand from Spruce Pine. After a few test runs, Roberts ordered thirteen boxcars to be delivered to Georgia. More than four thousand tons of sand have been delivered over the past forty years. In addition to being installed at Augusta and Linville, the sand is also at Mount Mitchell Golf Club, Cape Fear National Golf Club and even the home course of Tiger Woods in Florida.[234]

PARKWAY PLAYHOUSE

It was 1935 and local Burnsville hotel operator Rush Wray started talking about a summer theater in town. That theater opened a year later and ran for three years, before closing "for a lack of nourishment." But Rush kept talking, and Professor W.B. Harrell, staying at the Nu-Wray Inn, recommended

Bob Armstrong and Carl Ridge stand outside the Parkway Playhouse, Burnsville, October 1949. *State Archives of North Carolina.*

that Wray talk to P.W.R. Taylor of the drama department at the Women's College of the University of North Carolina, now UNC–Greensboro. Wray did just that, raising more than $2,000 to renovate the old Burnsville High School gymnasium building in town. In 1947, the Parkway Playhouse was born. For a number of years, the theater was operated by the college as a summer program. In the 1980s, Parkway Playhouse was operated by the University of Miami. In the 1990s, the theater became independent.[235]

MAYLAND COMMUNITY COLLEGE AND THE EARTH TO SKY PARK

A popular television program in 1966 started with, "Space, the final frontier...." No rocket ships are leaving the Toe River Valley, but visitors can explore not only our solar system but also our galaxy and neighboring galaxies at Mayland Community College's Earth to Sky Park.

Astronomy has always interested people in the Toe River Valley. Some residents have their own telescopes and backyard observatories, like the Willis Observatory in the Ledger community. Astronomy was taught at the Mount Mitchell Camp for Girls in the 1930s and has been a popular course offering at Mayland. However, Mayland offers the region something unique: the largest observational telescope in North Carolina and the largest telescope open to the public in the Southeast. Located at the former Energy Exchange, the site of an old mica mine and then landfill, the Earth to Sky Park features a thirty-four-inch Dobsonian telescope affectionately referred to as the "Sam Scope." The custom-made telescope was funded by a gift from the Samuel L. Philips Family Foundation. The Sam Scope is housed in the Bare Dark Sky Observatory, a gift from Warren and Larissa Bare. The telescope is historic, and the Bare Dark Sky Observatory, opened in 2017, was part of the first internationally certified Dark Sky park in North Carolina. Also located in the Earth to Sky Park is the Glenn and Carol Arthur Planetarium, which opened in June 2022.[236]

WOODY'S CHAIR SHOP

Having a craftsman in the community was always beneficial. The Woody family, some of the valley's earliest settlers, included such craftsmen. Wyatt Woody made chairs, wagons and tables, as did his son Henry Woody and his grandson, Arthur Woody. It was a true family business, with women working alongside men. The woodworking shop, in the Grassy Creek

Arthur Woody, with his daughter, Dixie, caned chairs at the Penland School. *Penland School of Crafts.*

section of Mitchell County, was water powered for many decades. In the early days, wagon- or sled-loads of chairs were taken down the mountain to sell in Marion, Forest City and Rutherfordton. The money was used to buy resources not produced on the farm, like sugar and coffee. The reputation of Woody's Chair Shop spread over time. When President John F. Kennedy's physician recommended a rocking chair to alleviate back pain, the order was sent to the shop, and at least one rocker was manufactured and sent to Washington. At the behest of Governor Terry Sandford, smaller chairs were made for JFK's children, Caroline and John Jr. The small chairs were in the White House throughout the Kennedy presidency and are now at the Kennedy Presidential Library in Boston. As of 2023, the old shop is up for sale.[237]

Chapter 30

MAKING SURE HISTORY
DOESN'T STAY HIDDEN

A Few Area Museums

While it can be a challenge to experience many of the historic sites and features of the region's hidden history, there are, fortunately, some great museums in the Toe River Valley. Each one tells part of the region's story, and each one has its own unique hidden history.

AVERY COUNTY HISTORICAL MUSEUM (Avery County). Opened in 1913, the Avery County Jail operated until 1970. The jail incarcerated prisoners, but it was also home to the jailer or sheriff and his family. During the push for local history during the national bicentennial, the Avery County Historical Museum opened in the old jail. The original cells are still upstairs, and there are numerous displays on local schools, the military, important people and local medicine, as well as a research room. Behind the museum are the restored 1917 Linville Depot and the ET&WNC Caboose 505, both of which are open for tours; they are the only remaining depot and caboose from the LRR.

BANNER HOUSE (Avery County). Constructed circa 1865 by Samuel Banner, the Banner House Museum demonstrates what life was like in the mountains of Western North Carolina in the mid- to late nineteenth century. On the grounds, a North Carolina Civil War Trail Marker discusses the Land of Goshen, a hideout for those seeking to escape from the area during the Civil War. Men, often escaped Union prisoners or dissidents, sheltered in this area until guided over the mountains into Tennessee. The Greater Banner Elk

The Avery County Historical Museum, in Newland, was once the Avery County Jail. *Author's collection.*

Heritage Foundation purchased, renovated and opened the Banner House Museum in 2007. The museum is open seasonally.

BEECH MOUNTAIN HISTORY MUSEUM (Avery County). The Beech Mountain History Museum endeavors to tell both the histories of the stalwart families of old Beech who carved out a living in the mountain slopes and those who came afterward to ski or have summer homes. Visitors can find information on the area's logging railroads, the Carolina Caribbean Corporation and the Land of Oz. The museum is open seasonally.

GRANDFATHER MOUNTAIN (Avery County). The Wilson Center for Nature Discovery contains information on Grandfather Mountain, including a mineral cave, migration mapping of birds, trees and extreme weather. On the second floor of the Top Shop, near the Mile High Swinging Bridge, is the Hugh Morton photo gallery. Exhibits include a history of Grandfather Mountain, construction of the bridge, Morton's World War II service and the Grandfather Mountain Highland Games.

MUSEUM OF NORTH CAROLINA MINERALS (Mitchell County). Located in the Spruce Pine Mining District, the Museum of North Carolina Minerals showcases the rich and diverse minerals that have been mined in the area. The museum, which opened in 1955, is located right off the Blue Ridge

The McBee Museum in Bakersville is housed in a circa 1890s building next door to the Mitchell County Courthouse. *Author's collection*.

Parkway. The site is also on the path of the Overmountain Victory Trail and hosts an encampment every October telling the story of the Overmountain Men and their march toward Kings Mountain.

MITCHELL COUNTY HISTORICAL MUSEUM/THE MCBEE MUSEUM (Mitchell County) Constructed in the 1890s, the McBee Museum has played many different roles in local history, including a general store, doctor's office, pharmacy and a law office. The building sits beside the historic courthouse in Bakersville and, in 1995, was given to the Mitchell County Historical Society, which uses the structure to tell the story of Mitchell County's history.

MOUNT MITCHELL STATE PARK (Yancey County). Mount Mitchell became the first state park in North Carolina in 1915. The park contains 4,789 acres, including the highest peak in eastern North America. There are hiking trails and a picnic area. Telling the story of Elisha Mitchell, Thomas Clingman and Big Tom Wilson is a museum that also contains displays on the natural history of the area and the logging that once took place. One special feature is the tombstone that once graced the grave of Professor Mitchell. The professor's grave is still situated on the top of the mountain, with an observation deck nearby.

Burnsville's circa 1840 McElroy House is the oldest site open as a museum in the Toe River Valley. *Author's collection.*

RUSH WRAY MUSEUM (Yancey County). The Yancey History Association was formed in 1979 and, in 1989, purchased the circa 1840 McElroy House, along with a 1920s gas station in Burnsville, with plans to conserve the structures. The gas station became the Chamber of Commerce/Visitor's Center, and the McElroy House was opened to the public in 1999. Next door is the Yancey County History and Genealogical Library. Much of the McElroy House is set up to represent the 1860s, while the annex next door contains not only the library but also many displays on local history. A special treat is the bell from USS *Burns*, a Fletcher-class World War II destroyer named for Otway Burns.

NOTES

Introduction

1. Jason Deyton, "The Toe River Valley to 1865" (master's thesis, University of North Carolina–Chapel Hill, 1931), 1.

Chapter 1

2. John Preston Arthur, *Western North Carolina: A History* (Johnson City, TN: Overmountain Press, 1914, 1996), 213; S.M. Dugger, *The Balsam Groves of the Grandfather Mountain* (Banner Elk, NC, 1934), 1,974.
3. "Naming of Places in the Carolinas," *Southern and Western Magazine and Review* 2, no. 6 (December 1845): 374.

Chapter 2

4. James Mooney, *History, Myths, and Sacred Formulas of the Cherokee* (Nashville, TN: Charles and Randy Elder-Booksellers, 1982), 527; Carolyn Sakowski, *Touring the East Tennessee Backroads* (Winston-Salem, NC: John F. Blair, 2007), 63.
5. Mooney, *History, Myths, and Sacred Formulas*, 542.

Chapter 3

6. John P. Arthur, *A History of Watauga County, North Carolina* (Richmond, VA: Everett Waddey Company, 1915), 16; Lyman Draper, *King's Mountain and Its Heroes*

(Cincinnati, OH: P.G. Thomson, 1881), 445; *Lenoir Topic*, June 24, 1885; Lloyd Bailey, *The Heritage of the Toe River Valley*, vol. 4 (Marceline, MO: Walsworth Publishing Company, 2004), 172.

7. William Saunders, *The Colonial Records of North Carolina*, vol. 10 (Raleigh, NC: Joseph Daniels, 1890), 712–13.

8. Max Dixon, *The Wataugans* (Johnson City, TN: Overmountain Press, 1976, 1989), 56, 61; Hugh F. Rankin, *North Carolina in the American Revolution* (Raleigh, NC: Division of Archives and History, 1959), 41; Robert Dunkerly, *The Battle of Kings Mountain* (Charleston, SC: The History Press, 2007), 43, 45, 91.

9. Draper, *King's Mountain and Its Heroes*, 177–80.

10. William Powell, *North Carolina: Through Four Centuries* (Chapel Hill: University of North Carolina Press, 1989), 199–200; *Tri-County News*, September 13, 1951.

11. *Kentucky Gazette*, June 19, 1823; Herbert Hoover address at Kings Mountain, October 7, 1930, the American Presidency Project; Theodore Roosevelt, *The Winning of the West* (New York: Review of Reviews Company, 1910), 2:286; Draper, *King's Mountain and Its Heroes*, 177.

12. Deyton, "Toe River Valley to 1865," 432.

Chapter 4

13. Timothy Silver, *Mount Mitchell and the Black Mountains* (Chapel Hill: University of North Carolina Press, 2003); Charles Hudson, ed., *The Juan Pardo Expeditions* (Tuscaloosa: University of Alabama Press, 1990).

14. Helen Norman and Patricia Page, *Yellow Mountain Road* (n.p.: CreateSpace, 2014) xiii; Jerry L. Cross, "Center of the Mountain Heartland: A Historical Profile of Yancey County" (North Carolina Division of Archives and History, 1994), 18; Arthur, *Western North Carolina*, 232.

15. *Fayetteville Weekly Observer*, December 7, 1831; *The Harbinger*, January 16, 1834; Cross, "Center of the Mountain Heartland," 19.

16. *Fayetteville Weekly Observer*, December 8, 1856; February 9, 1857.

17. *Charlotte Democrat*, November 30, 1858; *Semi-Weekly Standard* November 24, 1860. The fable that Mitchell County was created overnight in early 1861 was popularized by Muriel Sheppard in *Cabins in the Laurel* (Chapel Hill: University of North Carolina Press, 1935, 1991), 56.

18. Claudia McGough, *Childsville: Old Times Are Not Forgotten* (n.p., 2003), 146.

19. *Charlotte News*, February 21, 1907; *The Robesonian*, January 28, 1909.

Chapter 5

20. *News and Observer*, June 21, 1959; Lowell Presnell, *Mines, Miners, and Minerals of Western North Carolina* (Alexander, NC: Land of Sky Books, 2004), 13.

21. John Waite, *The Blue Ridge Stemwinder* (Johnson City, TN: Overmountain Press, 2003), 4–10.

22. Presnell, *Mines, Miners, and Minerals*, 42; W.B. Phillips, "Mica Mining in North Carolina," *Journal of the Elisha Mitchell Scientific Society* 2, no. 5 (July–December 1888): 73–97.

23. Anita P. Davis, *North Carolina and World War II: A Documentary Portrait* (Jefferson, NC: McFarland, 2015), 52–3; *News and Observer*, May 17, 1942; Bill Sharpe, "Mine Is High; So Is Mica," *The State* (December 13, 1952): 16–17.

24. *Johnson City Press*, May 9, 1952; *Tampa Bay Times*, September 13, 1956.

25. Presnell, *Mines, Miners, and Minerals*, 79.

26. Ibid., 55–60.

27. Robert J. Schabilion, *Down the Crabtree* (n.p.: Authorhouse, 2009), 128–29; Presnell, *Mines, Miners, and Minerals*, 73, 95; *Mountain Express*, February 26, 2016.

Chapter 6

28. Silver, *Mount Mitchell*, 58; Jonathan Bennett and David Biddix, *Mount Mitchell* (Charleston, SC: Arcadia Publishing, 2005), 9.

29. Silver, *Mount Mitchell*, 78–84; Kemp Battle, *Diary of a Geological Tour by Dr. Elisha Mitchell* (Chapel Hill: University of North Carolina Press, 1905), 52.

30. Silver, *Mount Mitchell*, 78–88.

31. Thomas E. Jeffrey, *Thomas Lanier Clingman: Fire Eater from Carolina Mountains* (Athens: University of Georgia Press, 1999), 143, 146.

32. William Powell, *North Carolina Gazetteer* (Chapel Hill: University of North Carolina Press, 2010), 352, 362; Bennett and Biddix, *Mount Mitchell*, 24; *Weekly Pioneer*, April 18, 1872.

33. Bennett and Biddix, *Mount Mitchell*, 12–13, 15; *Charlotte Democrat*, April 9, 1872; S. Kent Schwarzkopf, *A History of Mt. Mitchell and the Blacks* (Raleigh: North Carolina Office of Archives and History, 1985), 79; Silver, *Mount Mitchell*, 199.

34. Bennett and Biddix, *Mount Mitchell*, 37.

35. Schwarkopf, *History of Mt. Mitchell*, 85; Silver, *Mount Mitchell*, 137, 138.

36. Silver, *Mount Mitchell*, 164; Marci Spencer, *Pisgah National Forest: A History* (Charleston, SC: The History Press, 2014), 71.

37. Silver, *Mount Mitchell*, 142; Schwarkopf, *History of Mt. Mitchell*, 90.

Chapter 7

38. *Spirt of the Age*, April 6, 1853; *Rowan Whig and Western Advocate*, October 7, 1853; *Weekly Standard*, October 4, 1854; *North Carolina Teacher* 4, no. 2 (October 1886): 100.

39. *Charlotte News*, September 26, 1915; Arthur, *Western North Carolina*, 446.

40. *Asheville Daily Gazette*, June 21, 1899; *Biblical Reporter*, July 19, 1899.

41. Lloyd Bailey, *A History of the Methodist Church in the Toe River Valley* (Burnsville, NC: Celo Printing, 1986), 192, 219; Daniel J. Whitener, *History of Watauga County* (Boone, NC: Souvenir of the Watauga County Centennial, n.d.), 78–81.

42. *Minutes of the Yancey Baptist Association*, 1899, 1900, 1901; *Charlotte Daily Observer*, February 22, 1903; National Register of Historic Places registration form.
43. *Asheville Weekly Citizen*, May 19, 1903; December 16, 1920; December 3, 1922; June 6, 1926; December 9, 1927; *Charlotte Observer*, May 27, 1927; Yancey History Association, *Images of Yancey* (Burnsville, NC: Yancey History Association, 1993), 64; *Hearings Before a Special Committee to Investigate Communist Activities* (Washington, D.C.: U.S. Government Printing Office, 1930), 264; *Charlotte Observer*, November 20, 1929.
44. *Greensboro Daily News*, April 30, 1907; *News-Herald*, October 1, 1908; *Charlotte News*, October 1, 1908; *News and Observer*, February 3, 1909; *Charlotte Observer*, May 31, 1925; *Watauga Democrat*, January 27, 1927, July 21, 1927; *Kingsport Times*, January 2, 1930.
45. *Morning Press*, October 25, 1933; *Asheville Citizen-Times*, November 25, 1941; *The State* 21, no. 8 (July 25, 1953): 5.

Chapter 8

46. *Southern Citizen*, February 25, 1837.
47. Noel Yancey, "Frankie Silver Murder Case," in *Encyclopedia of North Carolina*, ed. William Powell (Chapel Hill: University of North Carolina Press, 2006), 1,036.
48. *Lenoir Topic*, March 24, May 5, 1886; *Southern Citizen*, February 25, 1837.

Chapter 9

49. *Asheville News*, November 13, 1856; *Western Sentinel*, November 16, 1860; John L. Cheney Jr., ed., *North Carolina Government, 1585–1979: A Narrative and Statistical History* (Raleigh: North Carolina Department of the Secretary of State, 1981), 1,397–1,401.
50. Noble Tolbert, *The Papers of John W. Ellis*, 2 vols. (Raleigh, NC: State Department of Archives and History, 1964), 2:510–15; *Weekly Raleigh Register*, November 23, 1860; *Charlotte Democrat*, December 22, 1860; Fronts Johnston, *Zebulon B. Vance Letters* (Raleigh, NC: State Department of Archives and History, 1963), 71–72, 88, 92.
51. *Fayetteville Weekly Observer*, February 25, 1861; *Charlotte Democrat*, March 12, 1861; Deyton, "Toe River Valley to 1865," 460; John McCormick, *Personnel of the Convention of 1861* (Chapel Hill: University of North Carolina Press, 1900), 66–67.
52. J. Carlyle Sitterson, *The Secession Movement in North Carolina* (Raleigh: University of North Carolina Press, 1939), 246–97; Weymouth Jordan, et al., *North Carolina Troops, 1861–1865: A Roster*, 21 vols. (Raleigh: North Carolina Division of Archives and History, 1961–present), 4:317–31, 6:28–37.
53. Jordan, *North Carolina Troops*, 8:246–55, 286–92, 300–305, 14:275–89.
54. Ibid., 2:348–54; 14:324–43, 358–74, 396–404.

55. Shepherd Dugger, *War Trails of the Blue Ridge* (Banner Elk, NC, 1932), 203, "The Banner Brothers of Co. B, 4th TN Cav (USA)," online, https://sites.rootsweb.com/~tn4cav/banner1.html.

56. *Asheville News*, March 27, 1862; Deyton, "Toe River Valley to 1865," 462–63; John W. McElroy to Zebulon B. Vance, July 13, 1863, and J. Metcalf to Zebulon B. Vance, July 6, 1863; Governor's Papers, NCDAH; *Fayetteville Observer*, October 8, 1863.

57. Matthew W. Brown and Michael W., eds, *North Carolina Troops, 1861–1865: A Roster* (Raleigh, NC: Office of Archives and History, 2022), 21:195–330.

58. Bailey, *Heritage of the Toe River Valley*, 1:55; Malone Young, *Latchpins of the Lost Cove* (n.p., Latchpin Press, 1987), 6; "Spotlighting School and Community History: Bee Log Honeybee Historians," (n.p., n.d.), 24; *Tri-County News*, December 24, 1953; Avery County Historical Museum, *Avery County Heritage* (Banner Elk, NC: Puddingstone Press, 1976), 1:22; Martha A. Pyatte, *The Pyatte Family of Western North Carolina* (Banner Elk, NC: Puddingstone Pres, 1977), 101–2.

59. Robert V. Blackstock to Vance, April 18, 1864, Governor's Papers, NCDAH; *Asheville News*, April 21, 1864.

60. Michael C. Hardy, *Kirk's Civil War Raids Along the Blue Ridge* (Charleston, SC: The History Press, 2020), 97–105.

61. Dugger, *War Trails of the Blue Ridge*, 110–18.

62. Hardy, *Kirk's Civil War Raids*, 131–39.

63. *Weekly Standard*, November 30, 1864; *Fayetteville Semi-Weekly Observer*, December 8, 1864; Bailey, *Heritage of the Toe River Valley*, 8:64–69.

64. These numbers are based on a survey of the 1860 census conducted by Michael Ledford and the author.

65. *Lenoir Topic*, September 28, 1887.

Chapter 10

66. *Asheville Citizen-Times*, May 24, 1934, January 11, 1936; March 2, 1938; July 27, 1950.

67. Victoria Logue, *Guide to the Blue Ridge Parkway* (Birmingham, AL: Menasha Ridge Press, 2010), 95.

68. *Charlotte Observer*, July 27, 1925.

69. *Asheville Citizen-Times*, September 28, 1949.

Chapter 11

70. *Fayetteville Semi-Weekly Observer*, June 26, 1854; *Asheville News*, August 15, 1855.

71. Waite, *Blue Ridge Stemwinder*, 20–30.

72. Johnny Graybeal, *Along the ET&WNC*, vol. 3 (Hickory, NC: Tar Heel Press, 2002), 3:78–79, 92–93; I. Harding Hughes, *Valle Crucis: A History of an Uncommon Place* (n.p.: Bookcrafters, 1995), 89.

73. Graybeal, *Along the ET&WNC*, 3:93.

74. Waite, *Blue Ridge Stemwinder*, 65.

75. *Asheville Citizen*, February 28, 1899.

76. Waite, *Blue Ridge Stemwinder*, 236–37; Graybeal, *Along the ET&WNC*, 3: 103–55.

77. *Raleigh Daily Telegraph*, February 23, 1871; *Charlotte Democrat*, April 11, 1871, June 5, 1885; *Charlotte Observer*, April 19, 1881; *Gastonia Gazette*, January 27, 1888.

78. *Semi-Weekly Citizen*, March 22, 1901; *Morning Post*, July 13, 1901.

79. *Morning Post*, February 25, 1901.

80. *Asheville Citizen*, January 5, 1887; *Asheville Democrat*, October 17, 1889.

81. *News and Observer*, February 14, 1883; *Asheville Weekly Citizen*, June 30, 1883.

82. *Morning Post*, March 12, 1905; *Greensboro Patriot*, August 23, 1905.

83. *News and Observer*, February 27, 1885; *Asheville Citizen-Times*, April 24, 1887; *Charlotte Democrat*, November 4, 1887.

84. *Watauga Democrat*, November 12, 1896.

85. *Asheville Gazette-News*, September 19, 1910; Thomas Fetters, *Logging Railroads of the Blue Ridge and Smoky Mountains* (n.p.: Timbertimes Inc., 2007), 136–37.

86. *Asheville Democrat*, July 7, 1892.

87. *Asheville Democrat*, December 19, 1889.

88. James Goforth, *Building the Clinchfield* (n.p.: Gem Publishers, 1989), 23.

89. *News and Observer*, January 31, 1903; *Knoxville Sentinel*, August 24, 1903; *The Comet*, November 12, 1903; *Asheville Citizen-Times*, January 9, 2011; Bailey, *Heritage of the Toe River Valley*, 1:15; Fetters, *Logging Railroads*, 154.

90. *Asheville Citizen*, March 4, 1911; March 22, 1911; March 28, 1911; William S. Cannon, "The South Toe Rambler," *Trains Magazine* (August 1974): 36–40.

91. *Asheville Citizen-Times*, March 21, 1915; *Johnson City Staff*, March 26, 1915; *Wilmington Morning Star*, April 12, 1915.

92. Bailey, *Heritage of the Toe River Valley*, 1:22.

93. *Charlotte Observer*, April 11, 1916; *Knoxville Sentinel*, April 25, 1905; Fetters, *Logging Railroads*, 108.

94. Fetters, *Logging Railroads*, 155.

Chapter 12

95. *Asheville Citizen Times*, January 16, 1931; June 9, 1935.

96. *North Carolina Spectator and Western Advertiser*, August 6, 1830.

97. Mitchell County Historical Society, "Bandana," https://mitchellnchistory.org/2017/01/15/bandana.

98. Hardy, *Avery County Place Names*, 11–12.

99. Silver, *Mount Mitchell*, 95, 117, 119.

100. Ibid.

101. Mitchell County Historical Society, "About Mitchell County," https://mitchellnchistory.org/about-mitchell-county/places.

102. Mooney, *History, Myths, and Sacred Formulas*, 324.

103. Mitchell County Historical Society, "Clarissa," https://mitchellnchistory. org/2018/12/10/clarissa.

104. Hardy, *Avery County Place Names*, 25.

105. *Asheville Citizen-Times*, May 31, 1953.

106. Hardy, *Avery County Place Names*, 28.

107. Ken Randolph, message to the author, November 10, 2022.

108. *Asheville Citizen-Times*, May 31, 1953.

109. Mitchell County Historical Society, "Huntdale," https://mitchellnchistory. org/2017/01/16/huntdale.

110. Hardy, *Avery County Place Names*, 41.

111. *Asheville Citizen-Times*, May 31, 1953.

112. Mitchell County Historical Society, "Kona," https://mitchellnchistory. org/2018/12/10/kona.

113. Powell, *North Carolina Gazetteer*, 296.

114. *Asheville Citizen-Times*, May 31, 1953.

115. Hardy, *Avery County Place Names*, 45.

116. Mitchell County Historical Society, "Little Switzerland," https:// mitchellnchistory.org/2019/01/20/little-switzerland.

117. Powell, *North Carolina Gazetteer*, 314.

118. Christy A. Smith, *Lost Cove, North Carolina: Portrait of a Vanished Appalachian Community, 1864–1957* (Jefferson, NC: McFarland and Company, 2021).

119. Horton Cooper, *Avery County and Its People* (n.p., n.d.), 67.

120. Mitchell County Historical Society, "Minpro," https://mitchellnchistory. org/2018/12/10/minpro-2.

121. Hardy, *Avery County Place Names*, 51.

122. "Naming of Places in the Carolinas," *Southern and Western Magazine and Review* 2, no. 6 (December 1845): 374.

123. Mitchell County Historical Society, "About Mitchell County."

124. *Yancey Journal*, September 25, 1975.

125. Horton Cooper, "Things of Interest in Avery County," *The State* (January 15, 1949): 8.

126. Mitchell County Historical Society, "Poplar Hollow and Poplar Creek," https://mitchellnchistory.org/2018/12/10/poplar-hollow-poplar-creek.

127. *Asheville Citizen-Times*, May 31, 1953.

128. Ibid., "Red Hill," https://mitchellnchistory.org/2017/02/16/red-hill.

129. Mitchell County Historical Society, "Relief," https://mitchellnchistory. org/2017/01/07/relief.

130. Jennifer Bauer, *Roan Mountain*: *A Passage of Time* (Johnson City, TN: Overmountain Press, 1997), 1–2.

131. Ibid.; Charles Lanman, "Novelties of Southern Scenery," *Appleton's Journal of Literature, Science and Art* 2 (1869): 1, 296, 327.

132. Cooper, *Avery County and Its People*, 99.

133. David Biddix and Chris Hollifield, *Spruce Pine* (Charleston, SC: Arcadia Publishing, 2009), 9.

134. Mitchell County Historical Society, "Tipton Hill," https://mitchellnchistory. org/2019/01/20/tipton-hill-2.
135. Powell, *North Carolina Gazetteer*, 524.
136. *Greensboro Daily News*, August 16, 1925; Cooper, *Avery County and Its People*, 100.

Chapter 13

137. *Manchester Evening News*, January 4, 1893; *Asheville Citizen-Times*, January 4, 1893; *Times Leader*, January 4, 1893; *Evening World-Herald*, January 5, 1893.
138. *Evening World-Herald*, January 5, 1893.
139. Ibid.

Chapter 14

140. Les M. Brown and Joyce Compton Brown, "Riding the Rail to Legend: The North Cove 'Tally War' as Show of Force, as Manipulated Account, as Oral History," *Journal of Appalachian Studies* 4, no. 2 (Fall 1998): 225–38; *News and Observer*, February 15, 1922; May 25, 1922; *Statesville Record and Landmark*, July 16, 1923; *Asheville Citizen*, June 8, 1922.
141. Tom Rusher, *Until He Is Dead: Capital Punishment in Western North Carolina History* (Boone, NC: Parkway Publishers, 2003), 19; *Asheville Citizen-Times*, September 30, 1923.
142. *The Item*, September 28, 1923; *Asheville Citizen-Times*, September 28, 1923; September 29, 1923; Rusher, *Until He Is Dead*, 18.
143. *Charlotte Observer*, September 29, 1923; *Lincoln Journal Star*, September 29, 1923; Rusher, *Until He Is Dead*, 14; *Spartanburg Journal*, September 29, 1923; *Selma Times Journal*, September 30, 1923.
144. *Asheville Citizen-Times*, October 2, 1923; October 8, 1923.
145. *Asheville Citizen-Times*, October 24, 1923; *News and Observer*, October 22, 1923; Rusher, *Until He Is Dead*, 27.
146. Sondra Wilson, *In Search of Democracy: The NAACP Writings of James Weldon, Walter White and Roy Wilkins* (New York: Oxford University Press, 1999), 52; Doug McGuinn, *The Railroad to Nowhere* (Boone, NC: Bamboo Books, 2009), 34; Elliot Jaspin, *Buried in the Bitter Waters* (n.p.: Basic Books, 2008), 206–7.

Chapter 15

147. Bauer, *Roan Mountain*, 81–112; Allen Cook, *In the Shadow of the Roan: Stories from Days Long Past* (n.p.: Chestnut Ridge Publishing, 2021), 19.
148. *Asheville Citizen-Times*, March 1, 1917; August 7, 1948.
149. Judy Carson and Terry McKinney, *Altapass* (Charleston, SC: Arcadia Publishing, 2005), 8, 50, 52; *Bristol Herald Courier*, June 28, 1910; *Bristol Herald Courier*, July 1, 1911; *Asheville Citizen-Times*, July 13, 1913; *Chattanooga Daily Times*, May 28, 1916; *Tampa Tribune*, May 16, 1926; *Knoxville Journal*, May 19, 1926.

150. *Johnson City Staff-News*, April 21, 1930; *Elizabethton Star*, February 28, 1931; *Johnson City Chronicle*, October 25, 1934; May 26, 1939; *Johnson City Press*, January 19, 2004.

151. *Charlotte Observer*, June 23, 1926; June 13, 1928; *Johnson City Chronicle*, June 15, 1928; July 2, 1931; August 8, 1931; *Asheville Citizen-Times*, August 10, 1930.

152. *Avery Journal*, April 10, 1986; Howard E. Covington Jr., *Linville: A Mountain Home for 100 Years* (Linville, NC: Linville Resorts Inc., 1992), 22, 84–85.

153. *Marion Record*, November 1, 1894; *Newark Advance*, May 18, 1956; "The Grand Dame: Refreshed and Restored, the Nu-Wray Inn Still Holds On to Its Storied Past," *WNC Magazine* (November 2010).

154. *Asheville Citizen-Times*, August 13, 1939; August 10, 1952; Biddix and Hollifield, *Spruce Pine*, 12, 126.

Chapter 16

155. McGough, *Childsville*, 105.

156. Ibid., 97; *Semi-Weekly Standard*, July 11, 1857.

157. McGough, *Childsville*, 106, 111–56; *Raleigh Register*, January 8, 1862; Arthur, *Western North Carolina*, 201.

158. McGough, *Childsville*, 97.

Chapter 17

159. Powell, *North Carolina*, 481.

160. *Charlotte News*, January 18, 1931; *Asheville Citizen-Times*, August 10, 1931; August 30, 1932; Bessie Hoyt, *Come When the Timber Turns* (Banner Elk, NC: Puddingstone Press, n.d.), 31.

161. *Asheville Citizen-Times*, January 12, 1933.

162. Anita Davis, *North Carolina during the Great Depression* (Jefferson, NC: McFarland, 2003), 38; Silver, *Mount Mitchell*, 182–83; Harley Jolley, *That Magnificent Army of Youth and Peace* (Raleigh: North Carolina Office of Archives and History, 2007), 77–79; Peter Barr, *Hiking North Carolina's Lookout Towers* (Winston-Salem, NC: John F. Blair, 2008), 247–49, 257, 258.

163. *Marion Progress*, August 15, 1935; *Asheville Citizen-Times*, August 17, 1935; February 4, 1940.

Chapter 18

164. *News and Observer*, December 7, 1934.

165. *Charlotte Observer*, August 22, 1970; *Asheville Citizen-Times*, August 24, 1970.

166. History of the North Carolina Christmas Tree Industry, https://christmastrees. ces.ncsu.edu/christmastrees-history-of-the-north-carolina-christmas-tree-industry.

167. *Asheville Citizen-Times*, October 31, 1971; October 29, 1972; December 2, 1993.

Chapter 19

168. *Charlotte Observer*, January 18, 1937; *News and Observer*, January 8, 1940.

169. John Hairr, "Skiing," in *Encyclopedia of North Carolina History*, ed. William Powell (Chapel Hill: University of North Carolina Press, 2006), 1,039–40; *Kingsport Times-News*, October 15, 1989.

170. *Asheville Citizen-Times*, December 17, 1982; *Charlotte Observer*, December 15, 2010.

171. Tim Hollis, *The Land of Oz* (Charleston, SC: The History Press, 2016), 7, 13; *Asheville Citizen-Times*, October 1, 1999.

172. *Asheville Citizen-Times*, August 1, 1937; December 19, 1937; Biddix and Hollifield, *Spruce Pine*, 102–3.

173. *Yancey Journal*, August 30, 1962; April 20, 1967.

174. Covington, *Linville*, 27, 36–37, 55; Jennifer Laughlin, *Roan Mountain: A Passage of Time* (Winston-Salem, NC: John F. Blair, 1991), 85; *Charlotte Observer*, November 23, 1930; *Watauga Democrat*, February 19, 1914; *Asheville Citizen-Times*, September 3, 1914; July 7, 1933; *Tampa Tribune*, August 2, 1941.

175. *Asheville Citizen-Times*, March 20, 1938; *Yancey Record*, October 21, 1948.

Chapter 20

176. Francis M. Hamrick, "The Movie People Loved in Pensacola," *The State* (April 1973): 16–18.

177. *Herald-Sun*, May 31, 1974.

178. *Avery Journal*, October 15, 22; November 5, 1987.

179. Richard Federici, *On the Trail of the Last of the Mohicans* (Marion, NC: Mohican Press, 2016), 79, 85, 109.

180. Connie Nelson, *Film Junkie's Guide to North Carolina* (Winston-Salem, NC: John F. Blair, 2004), 356.

Chapter 21

181. Rudy Abramson and Jean Haskell, eds., *Encyclopedia of Appalachia* (Knoxville: University of Tennessee Press, 2006), 769, 771.

182. *Asheville Citizen-Times*, June 11, 2003; *Charlotte Observer*, July 16, 1933; Sheila Bumgarner, "Penland School of Crafts," in *Encyclopedia of North Carolina*, ed. William Powell (Chapel Hill: University of North Carolina Press, 2006), 877.

Chapter 22

183. Powell, *North Carolina*, 445; Howard Covington, *A Legacy of Caring: The First Hundred Years of Crossnore School* (n.p.: Quality Books Inc., 2012), 11–14.

184. Avery County Historical Museum, *Avery County Heritage* (Banner Elk, NC: Puddingstone Press, 1986), 4:22; Covington, *Legacy of Caring*, 30–33.

185. Covington, *Legacy of Caring*, 43, 45, 59, 119.
186. *Asheville Citizen-Times*, January 15, 1962.
187. *Statesville Record and Landmark*, May 3, 1951.

Chapter 23

188. Reuben Thwaites, *Early Western Travels*, vol. 3 (Cleveland, OH: Arthur H. Clark Company, 1904), 56; Dugger, *Balsam Groves of Grandfather Mountain*, 260–63.
189. Laughlin, *Roan Mountain*, 50–51; Silver, *Mount Mitchell*, 65.
190. George Ellison, *High Vistas: An Anthology of Nature Writing from Western North Carolina and the Great Smoky Mountains* (Charleston, SC: The History Press, 2008), 44; Joseph Ewan and Nesta Ewan, "John Lyon, Nurseryman and Plant Hunter, and His Journal, 1799–1814," *Transactions of the American Philosophical Society* 53, no. 2 (1963), 1–69.
191. Ellison, *High Vistas*, 50; Laughlin, *Roan Mountain*, 52.
192. A. Hunter Dupree, *Asa Gray, 1810–1888* (Cambridge, MA: Belknap Press of Harvard University Press, 1959), 97, 409.
193. Laughlin, *Roan Mountain*, 182.
194. Ellison, *High Vistas*, 107–8.

Chapter 24

195. *Wilmington Messenger*, February 13, 1897; *Union Republican*, February 18, 1897.
196. *Greensboro Daily News*, August 16, 1915; *Charlotte Observer*, October 19, 1918; *News and Observer*, November 2, 1920.
197. Anna Clark, "Biographical Sketch of Ella Clapp (Mrs. Ella St. Clair Thompson)," *Militant Women Suffragists—National Woman's Party* (Alexander, VA: Alexander Street Press, 2015), https://documents.alexanderstreet.com/d/1008297927; Derek Halsey, "Bulus B. Swift: An Activist for Women's and Children's Rights," *All About Women* 8 (2020).

Chapter 25

198. Arizona Hughes, *Aunt Zona's Web* (Banner Elk, NC: Puddingstone Press, 1976), 1–151 (summarized); Avery County Historical Museum, *Avery County Heritage* (Banner Elk, NC: Puddingstone Press, 1979), 2:132–35.
199. *Newton Enterprise*, February 13, 1908; Marcus B. Simpson Jr., "Thomas D. Wilson," ed. William Powell, *Biographical Dictionary of North Carolina*, 6 vols. (Chapel Hill: University of North Carolina Press, 1996), 6:78.
200. Bailey, *Heritage of the Toe River Valley*, 8:19–24.
201. Avery County Historical Museum, *Avery County Heritage*, 2:195–96; *Avery Journal-Times*, June 5, 2005.
202. *New York Times*, November 7, 1986; *Fort Worth Star-Telegram*, November 7, 1986.

203. *Avery Journal-Times*, July 11, 2015.
204. *Avery Journal-Times*, October 15, 2015; October 19, 2022.
205. *High Point Enterprise*, February 21, 1961.
206. Leslie Banner Cottingham and Carol Lowe Timblin, *The Bard of Ottaray: The Life, Letters and Documents of Shepherd Monroe Dugger* (Banner Elk, NC: Puddingstone Press, 1979).
207. *Avery Journal-Times*, March 29, 2016.
208. Bailey, *Heritage of the Toe River Valley*, 1:338–39.
209. *Charlotte Observer*, February 14, 2010.
210. *Avery Journal-Times*, April 5, 2017.
211. Charles W. Ray, U.S. Veterans Administration Pension Payment Cards, Record Group 15, National Archives; *Cecil Whig*, May 23, 2015; *Daily Oklahoman*, March 26, 1959.

Chapter 26

212. Jon Meacham, *American Lion: Andrew Jackson in the White House* (New York: Random House, 2008).
213. Hans L. Trefousse, *Andrew Johnson: A Biography* (New York: W.W. Norton, 1997).
214. *Asheville Daily Gazette*, September 10, 1902; *Morning Post*, December 11, 1904; *Greensboro Daily News*, April 16, 1912.
215. *Asheville Citizen-Times*, June 22, 1958.

Chapter 27

216. McGough, *Childsville*, 63, 71; Yancey History Association, *Images of Yancey*, 53.
217. Mary T. Sloop, *Miracle in the Hills* (New York: McGraw-Hill Book Company, 1953), 36; Yancey History Association, *Images of Yancey*, 54; Joann Thomas Croom, *No Work in the Grave: Life in the Toe River Valley* (Weaverville, NC: Dykeman Legacy Press, 2022), 254.
218. Bailey, *Heritage of the Toe River Valley*, 1:385.
219. Yancey History Association, *Images of Yancey*, 54; Howard E. Covington Jr., *Caring for One Another: The People and Hospitals that Became the Appalachian Regional Healthcare System* (n.p.: Verse Press, 2018), 14, 17; Mary Gilmer, *Panorama of Caring: The Story of Two Hospitals in Avery County, North Carolina* (Linville, NC: Avery Health Care System, 1999), 76–77, 101.
220. Gilmer, *Panorama of Caring*, 23, 116–23.
221. *News and Observer*, May 26, 1905; *Johnson City Press and Staff-News*, April 12, 1935; *Oregon Daily Journal*, January 15, 1911; *Charlotte Observer*, November 11, 1911; Carson and McKinney, *Altapass*, 75; *Raleigh Times*, December 6, 1910; *Asheville Citizen-Times*, February 26, 1960.
222. *Asheville Citizen-Times*, March 5, 1930; March 5, 1931; March 26, 1931; *News and Observer*, March 3, 1931; *Charlotte Observer*, November 15, 1955.

223. *Journal of the American Medical Association* 143, no. 1 (May 6, 1950): 78; *Asheville Citizen-Times*, November 4, 1971; *Mitchell News-Journal*, April 21, 2021.

224. Levi Branson, *Branson's North Carolina Business Directory* (Raleigh, NC: Levi Branson, Publisher, 1890), 719; *Asheville Citizen-Times*, October 22, 1931; January 17, 1932; September 11, 1998; *Yancey Record*, October 3, 1946.

225. *Asheville Citizen-Times*, June 16, 1928; July 4, 1953; *News and Observer*, March 8, 1929; *Journal of the House of Representatives of the General Assembly of North Carolina, Session 1929*, 497.

Chapter 28

226. *Asheville Citizen-Times*, May 24, 1901; *Morning Post*, May 25, 1901; *Greensboro Daily News*, July 20, 1916; *Wilmington Morning Star*, July 23, 1916; *News and Observer*, August 14, 1940; *Charlotte Observer*, August 14, 1940; *Yancey Records*, August 15, 1940.

227. *Marion Progress*, March 5, 1936; *Shelby Daily Star*, March 20, 1936; *Charlotte Observer*, March 19, 1936; January 7, 1960; March 14, 1993; *News and Observer*, March 19, 1936; March 15, 1960; *Asheville Citizen-Times*, January 21, 1960; *Johnson City Press*, March 15, 1993.

228. *Lenoir Topic*, August 26, 1885; *News and Observer*, July 21, 1926; *Charlotte Observer*, May 14, 1957.

229. Bruce Korn and Sandy Grisham, *Around Bakersville* (Charleston, SC: Arcadia Publishers, 2011), 52; *Avery Journal*, November 23, 2011.

Chapter 29

230. *Johnson City Press*, April 16, 1953; February 22, 1959; Bailey, *Heritage of the Toe River Valley*, 1:29.

231. *Annual Report of the Smithsonian Institute, 1918* (Washington, D.C.: Government Printing Office, 1919), 113.

232. Bennett and Biddix, *Mount Mitchell*, 107–8.

233. *Johnson City Press*, June 27, 1992; *Los Angeles Times*, April 22, 1999.

234. *Mitchell News Journal*, November 18, 2020; *Los Angeles Times*, November 11, 2020.

235. Bill Sharpe, "They Help Build North Carolina," *The State* (February 25, 1950): 8.

236. *Knoxville Journal*, April 21, 1935.

237. *Asheville Citizen-Times*, October 16, 1932; May 15, 1961; *Johnson City Press*, January 13, 1992; *Bailey News Leader*, April 25, 1996.

INDEX

North Toe River 10, 17, 20, 23, 28, 30,
    54, 61, 62, 66, 81, 83, 85, 94, 99,
    100, 117, 118, 119, 137, 143, 160,
    164, 165, 168, 177

P

Palmer, John B. 68
Penland, Milton P. 61
Penland, NC 36, 89
Pensacola, NC 10, 40, 99, 136, 163,
    169
Pineola, NC 66, 71, 81, 82, 90, 125,
    157, 158, 170
Plumtree, NC 10, 26, 28, 51, 52, 64,
    85, 99, 131, 136, 137, 143, 171
Poplar, NC 10, 65, 89, 99, 100

R

Red Hill, NC 63, 100
Roan Mountain 6, 16, 37, 68, 100,
    110, 127, 128, 135, 149, 150, 164,
    166, 179
Roaring Creek, NC 17, 18, 19, 23, 25,
    66, 100, 127, 155, 164

S

Silver, Frankie and Charlie 54
Sloop, Mary M. and Eustace 143, 144,
    145, 146, 169, 171, 172
South Toe River 10, 43
Spruce Pine, NC 31, 34, 35, 36, 62,
    73, 83, 85, 86, 89, 100, 104, 106,
    108, 112, 124, 131, 137, 153, 166,
    167, 173, 174, 177, 179, 183, 188

T

Tipton Hill, NC 100, 124
Tufts, Edgar 51, 170, 171

U

Unaka Mountains 7, 11, 181

W

Watauga County, NC 12, 17, 25, 68,
    81, 129, 161
Watauga River 11, 12, 17
Wilder, John T. 86, 94, 110
Wilson, Big Tom 38, 150, 155, 189
Wing, Charles H. 45
Wiseman, Lulu Belle and Scotty 131,
    160

Y

Yancey, Bartlett 25
Yancey County, NC 6, 10, 25, 26, 27,
    33, 34, 36, 40, 44, 49, 52, 59, 61,
    64, 72, 73, 77, 86, 89, 94, 95, 96,
    97, 99, 100, 101, 110, 118, 120,
    123, 124, 132, 135, 136, 153, 155,
    158, 169, 174, 175, 176, 177, 180,
    189, 190
Yellow Mountain 17, 19, 21, 25, 37,
    63, 66, 100, 101, 149, 155

ABOUT THE AUTHOR

Michael C. Hardy has a passion for North Carolina history. He's written about battles, pirates and mountains in books, blog posts and articles. His ancestors lived in Surry and Wilkes Counties, marching with Colonel Benjamin Cleveland to fight at the Battle of Kings Mountain. Since 1995, Michael has called the High Country home. He is a former board member of both the Yancey History Association and the Avery County Historical Museum and in 2010 was named the North Carolina Historian of the Year. When not researching and writing, he volunteers as an interpreter at historic sites.